Sexy Mamas

Keeping Your Sex Life Alive
While Raising Kids

Cathy Winks & Anne Semans

New World Library
Novato, California

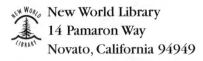 New World Library
14 Pamaron Way
Novato, California 94949

Copyright © 2004 by Cathy Winks and Anne Semans

Cover illustration: Juliette Borda

Library of Congress Cataloging-in-Publication Data
Winks, Cathy.
Sexy mamas : keeping your sex life alive while raising kids / Cathy Winks
and Anne Semans. — Rev. Ed.
p.   cm.
ISBN: 978-1-930722-27-9
1. Mothers—Sexual behavior. 2. Sex instructions for women.
3. Parenting. I. Semans, Anne. II. Title.

HQ46.W56 2004
306.874/3—dc22

ISBN: 978-1-930722-27-9

g New World Library is a proud member of the Green Press Initiative.

10   9   8   7   6   5   4   3   2

Table of Contents

Introduction

Moms Have Sex? Who Knew!

As soon as we started spreading the word about our idea for this book, we knew we were on to something. Parents instantly responded with curiosity, enthusiasm, and almost desperate nods of approval, while folks without kids looked politely puzzled. And who could blame them? Although volumes have been written about motherhood and sex, the two subjects lie on parallel tracks that rarely intersect. Parenting books never explore how a mother can expect her sex life to be transformed by the demands of child-rearing. Sex and relationship books for parents suggest tips for "keeping the flame alive" that depend on creating the illusion that you don't have kids. And neither ever address how honoring and enjoying your own sexuality through all the phases of your life sets a powerful example that enables your children to grow up to be responsible, sexually fulfilled adults.

Sexy Mamas reaches out to women who want to integrate the joys of a satisfying sex life with the joys of motherhood. We offer tips, anecdotes, and practical information about sex and parenting, supported by advice from medical experts, sex experts, and the most valuable experts of all—other mothers.

Mothers First

While we like to think that all parents can glean useful information and per-spective from this book, it is written first and foremost for mothers. We are unabashed in asserting that mothers need and deserve a book of their own—their sex lives have been invisible for far too long. Women simply aren't raised with a sense of entitlement to sexual expression, and mothers face the double-bind of social attitudes that deem maternity and sexuality mutually exclusive. Most mothers can testify that the desire for a fulfilling sex life didn't disappear when they had children, it simply got buried under an avalanche of conflicting demands on their time and attention. A woman's sex life undergoes significant changes from the moment she decides to have a child, and she has to navigate these changes with no more guidance than the occasional tidbit of information from a kindly nurse or relevant anecdote from a straight-shooting friend. The legions of mothers who visit sex-related discussion boards on parenting web sites—swapping stories on everything from waning desire to remaining kinky—reveal a profound hunger for an explicit discussion of sexual issues.

Ask a mom about her sex life, and you'll get responses ranging from, "Sex? What's that?" to "It's better than ever, but it took a lot of work." If you're partnered, you're probably not surprised by the statistic that parents living with children only spend about twenty minutes each week being intimate with each other. If you're single, perhaps you wonder how to be fully present for your kids without neglecting your own desires. You may have picked up this book because a sexual drought is making you long for "the good old days," or you may be curious to explore how your newfound maternal power and passion can enhance your sex life. Either way, we hope you'll find much in these pages that challenges your assumptions and fuels your desires.

The Moms Speak

We wanted our discussion of mothers' sexuality to reflect the concerns and experiences of a full spectrum of moms—married, single, heterosexual, lesbian, adoptive and biological—so we posted a survey in several places online, including Hip Mama's web site. Imagine our delight when over seven hundred impassioned and heartfelt responses poured in. We heard from women whose experiences ran the gamut of maternal sexuality—from sexually-confident fertility goddesses who were reveling in a sexual rebirth to mothers stymied by the practical and cultural restrictions on their sexuality. Their poignant and often humorous quotes appear throughout this book, and their comments guided our writing.

We owe a debt of gratitude to the moms who shared their thoughts—not just because they sacrificed some of their precious free time to contribute to our book—but because their stories reveal how every aspect of motherhood has sexual repercussions: from the roller coaster ride of fluctuating hormones to the challenges of prioritizing personal pleasure with children on the scene. It's our goal to take as comprehensive an approach as possible in affirming a mother's identity as a sexual being. Throughout this book, we refer to your sexual "partners": a neutral term we use deliberately, since exploring your sexuality with a long-term spouse or a short-term fling is equally valid.

Using This Book

Whether you're struggling with a shifting sexual self image, you're curious about why your sex drive flew the coop, or you're single and need tips for meeting people, you'll find help here. The early chapters deal with the core components that define a woman's relationship to her own sexuality, including sexual self-image, self-esteem, masturbation, desire, and communication. The later chapters deal with an array of obstacles to her love and sex life a mother may encounter, and include practical advice on how to make sex a priority, how to share the responsibility for a fulfilling sex life with a partner, how to manage a sex life when you're single, and how to expand your experience of sex. In order to inspire some creative change in your own life, we've sprinkled over one hundred easy-to-try Hot Tips throughout the book, all designed to help you embrace a bigger, better sexuality.

Who We Are

We're lifelong friends and colleagues motivated by the philosophy that everyone is entitled to a happy, healthy sex life. Together we've written two nonfiction sex guides that offer up-to-date information and practical advice on how to enjoy safe and satisfying sexual explorations. Our first book, *The Good Vibrations Guide to Sex*, was born out of our decade-long careers as vibrator saleswomen at San Francisco's women-owned erotic emporium, Good Vibrations. Our second book, *The Woman's Guide to Sex on the Web*, was inspired by our appreciation of the Internet's contribution to women's sexual empowerment and self-expression. Both endeavors gave us a provocative glimpse into the bedrooms of ordinary women and men of all ages and backgrounds.

In our lives and in our work, we're dedicated to furthering women's sexual emancipation. Anne wrote the on-line "Sex and Parenting" column for the popular magazine *Hip Mama* and is a regular contributor to the women's sexuality site Libida.com. She enjoys firsthand experience as the single mother of two young girls. Cathy is a health educator at The Sperm Bank of California, providing information and support to women and men who are building families through donor insemination. She lives with her partner, Becky, and their son.

As YOU Please

We realize that advice books, particularly parenting books, can make you feel like you're back in school struggling to keep up with homework assignments—after you've finished absorbing details relevant to one developmental stage, you take a breather, and then it's on to the next stage. If you or your child lag behind, you start to feel like a screw-up, or that you're missing out on some grand opportunities. The last thing we want is for readers of *Sexy Mamas* to feel inadequate as a result of our advice, or other mothers' experiences. We offer tools, information, and a lot of encouragement to explore your maternal sexuality, but please honor your own experience and explore at your own pace.

Most of all, we want to send you on your way with our thanks and praises. It takes courage and determination to challenge the cultural conditioning that mothers should practice self-sacrifice, rather than pursue their true sexual desires. We hope this book gives you the inspiration and the means to pursue a lifetime filled with sexual pleasure.

Note: An expanded version of this book entitled The Mother's Guide to Sex *was published in 2001 by Three Rivers Press.*

1

Why Moms
Make Better Lovers

*S*exy moms. Let's admit it, these two words don't exactly conjure up the same wealth of images as, say, "voluptuous vixens" or "smokin' hotties." Sure, you may have qualified as one of the latter before becoming a parent, but your new identity as somebody's mom trumps every identity you've had before. Why are moms desexualized? The reasons are complex—a cultural view of sex as dirty, a religious tradition that celebrates chaste motherhood, and a social system that demands maternal self-sacrifice. The irony that sex is what makes many women mothers in the first place probably isn't lost on you.

> The looks I get if I walk into a store like Victoria's Secret are hysterical! I feel like asking people if they know how my son got here in the first place. I'm no less a sexual being now then I was before my child. In fact, I feel like more of a sexual being now that I'm a mom. I mean, I created a whole other person in my body with the help of the person that I love! How much more sexual can you get?

This mother speaks for countless others—both biological and nonbiological—who have found that becoming parents inspires them with a new sexual confidence and vitality. A renewed respect for their bodies, an increased capacity for love, a powerful connection to humanity: these are the reasons women cite most often for the improved self-image that unites the best of their maternal and sexual selves.

Yet few mothers arrive at sexual independence without having had a bumpy ride en route. You, like many others, may have lost sight of your sexual self as a result of physical changes, logistical challenges, hormonal fluctuations, or negative messages from partners, friends, and strangers. We don't intend to suggest that if motherhood prompts a sabbatical from sex, you've somehow failed to "be all you can be." Everyone goes through natural cycles of sexual activity. But we are arguing that our identity as sexual beings is nonnegotiable, and that no one is ever justified in making you feel that motherhood and sexuality are mutually exclusive. Sexuality is the source of your creativity; it infuses you with love, energy, and a sense of well-being. It improves all your relationships, and makes you more human to your own children. Whether you're carving a new notch in the bedpost every night, or whether you can't remember the last time you got a little action—your erotic nature is your undeniable birthright.

The Challenges We Face

If it were so easy to seamlessly integrate our sexual and maternal selves, you probably wouldn't be reading this book right now. Every woman's self-image gets an overhauling in the transition to motherhood, and sexuality is just one of the aspects of your identity that is temporarily dismantled. It takes a while to complete a transformation that allows you to feel true to yourself; in fact, it's an ongoing process. Here are some of the common challenges to your post-baby sexual identity, which we'll revisit throughout the book.

Unattainable ideals

All moms experience a period when they're too tired to care how they look, and stained clothes dominate the wardrobe. Biological moms have the double-whammy of major physical changes, and some experience a certain disconnect around their dual-purpose bodies. When genitals or breasts are serving a utilitarian purpose, it's not always easy to see them as sexual.

> Breastfeeding and taking care of a small infant who lived IN MY BODY for nine months changed my perception of my sexual self. I thought of my body as more of a tool for a while, and so many things hurt physically for so long. I feel that just now, two years after the birth of my daughter, I have come full circle. I am able to separate

my sexual self from my parent self, and it feels like a great personal change, so healthy.

Now being the somewhat dumpy stay-at-home mom that I am, it's difficult to reconcile that with the sexy sweet young thang I once was. I'm learning to love myself as a GODDESS with the broad hips, low breasts and the incredible life experience that implies.

It doesn't help that media images of motherhood tend to swing between one extreme—down-and-out welfare moms—to the other—high-powered professional or celebrity moms, who are leading lives that are completely unattainable to the rest of us. The former are blamed for having a sex life, and the latter are praised for having a sex life. When *People* magazine ran a cover story on "Sexy Moms" several years ago, this quote was typical of the dozens of readers who complained.

How come being sexy means you must look like you never gave birth at all? Why can't round, curvy, real women and moms be considered sexy too?

Since most moms don't see themselves reflected in these images, they find the notion of sexy motherhood almost depressing. If motherhood means keeping a clean house and raising well-adjusted kids while looking like a million bucks, who wouldn't feel like a failure? And we're right to be suspicious of this house-of-wax version of sexy motherhood. With her glamorous, never-a-hair-out-of-place veneer, the twenty-first-century celebrity mom bears a certain suspicious resemblance to the perfect fifties housewife (she just gets a personal trainer and private nutritionist instead of a vacuum and blender).

Marriage manuals from the nineteen-thirties through the fifties emphasized that husbands and wives needed to prioritize their sex lives for the health and stability of the family. A wife's way of contributing to this otherwise laudable goal was to stay sexy and feminine and not to "let herself go," for fear that her neglected husband might be driven to stray. This was the same time period during which Freudian theories were widespread, and most middle-class American women knew that they were supposed to divest themselves of their immature attachment to clitoral stimulation and adopt a "mature" sexuality focused on vaginal intercourse; gynecologists of the day advised wives of "the advantage of innocent simulation of sex responsiveness," in other words, the advantage of faking orgasm![1]

Your parents may not have read these marriage manuals, but chances are good that they absorbed the philosophy that a good wife takes responsibility for her husband's sexual satisfaction—and that you inherited some version of this idea. Numerous retro parenting guides are still printed every year urging wives to sustain some kind of partner sex life come hell or high water. But who wants to sustain a sex life if her own sexual pleasure is secondary? Many mothers find that it takes some time after becoming a parent to get back in touch with their sex drive, and you'll be a lot more motivated to do so if the goal is exploring how your sexual responses may have changed—instead of focusing on "losing the baby weight" and greeting your hubby at the front door wearing nothing but Saran Wrap! Sure, we all want to retain our sexual attractiveness—for ourselves as well as our partners—but setting the bar unreasonably high can lead to a vicious cycle of self-loathing: we end up feeling undesirable, which inhibits our ability to project a sexual confidence that others might find attractive. The experience ends up confirming our suspicions that we've lost our sex appeal.

> I feel so gross and emotionally drained. I no longer appeal to men on the street, nobody takes a second look anymore. I feel old and haggard, like I am no fun anymore.

The challenges to your self-image won't all revolve around physical appearance. If your initial experience of motherhood isn't one of instinctive, effortless love and bonding, you may feel like a terrible fraud—but you should know that you're not alone. Communicating with other mothers—particularly in the anonymous, candid environment of on-line forums—can be hugely reassuring.

> I felt as though I had lost myself, and it was such an awful and scary feeling. I've only recently began to locate me again. I remember feeling as though the light that I had, which was so bright, was losing its strength. I felt like I was the only woman who wasn't absolutely ecstatic and in love with her baby. Oh yes, I love him dearly, but these feelings were real and weighed very heavily on my conscience.

Everyone wants a piece of Mom

It's easy to be so overwhelmed by the very real demands of motherhood that your sexuality is the last thing on your mind. For some, it's the sheer increase in responsibility that saps their sexual energy.

> I have a lot more insecurities now than I did before I was a mother—body issues, single mother issues, time and privacy issues, potential stepfather issues. It's hard to even view myself as a sexual being sometimes.

> My sense of self changed the day he was born. I was given tons more responsibility. I took on this "role" right from the beginning. I saw myself as a mother and a housekeeper. Sexual being was not on my list.

Other women are overwhelmed by the pressure to become the ultimate self-sacrificing mom, striving for an unrealistic and unhealthy ideal that society tends to shove down our throats.

> I had to struggle to hang on to the me who was me—as opposed to the MOM me. It is always a struggle for women, I think. So many demands, expectations, etc. So many perfectly coifed PTA moms wearing holiday theme sweaters and bright smiles.

Unless you actually are a celebrity mom (in which case we apologize for our snotty comments above) with a bevy of personal trainers, chefs, drivers, nannies, and assistants who can manage the mundane details of your life, you're bound to run into what we've dubbed "scarcity" issues. If you don't have enough time or energy to make sexual expression a possibility, let alone a priority, in your life, check out the Having It All chapter.

Double standards

We all inherit the same double standard around female sexuality. You and your partner may struggle with a fear that sex has the power to transform a sainted mother like you into a selfish, slutty whore. Even if your fears don't take such extreme forms, you've probably experienced at least a fleeting anxiety that the sexual activities you enjoyed before becoming a mother just aren't quite "appropriate" any more.

I felt that mothers couldn't be sexual—that the roles were pretty specific: mothers took care of the kids, mistresses took care of the fathers.

Mothering is not traditionally seen as a sexual role and I felt castrated! My hormones changed and I just didn't feel like a sexual person anymore. Moms are not sexy. They lactate. They make lunches. They clean the house and then they are supposed to transform at evening into this sexy thing for the husband's pleasure. I didn't transform at all. I just mothered.

My husband wants me to be more conservative now. He feels some of the things I wear are not suitable. I want to feel sexy again—it was always such a big part of me.

Then again, violating a taboo does have some erotic potential.

A lot of men find me more desirable—it's that whole "perfect mommy" by day, slut by night syndrome.

Many moms internalize the Madonna/whore double-bind so thoroughly that they begin to censor, not only their sexual activities, but their sexual fantasies, according to some unwritten rules regarding how to be a "good mom."

I no longer enjoy reading porn as I did occasionally before we became parents, and wish he wouldn't even bring it into the house, ditto with X-rated videos, they actually make me sick now.

I have heard many girlfriends say that they felt sex was too "dirty" after their children were born.

I sometimes feel guilty for thinking sexual thoughts, like as a mom I shouldn't feel that way.

By repressing your sexuality—and all its colorful kinkiness—you lose access to an important part of yourself. While you can't very well avoid experiencing anxieties that have been drummed into our collective consciousness for millennia, you can cultivate awareness of your self-censoring moments, and thereby open yourself up to a world of sexual self-discovery.

Sometimes I catch myself thinking that, because I'm a mom, I shouldn't be having the thoughts I have sometimes! Then I remind myself what BS that is.

Andrea O'Reilly, the founder of the Association of Research on Motherhood, theorizes that the source of our collective cultural uneasiness over sexually expressive mothers is that they are simply too powerful for men to deal with:

Women have power two ways, sexually and as mothers. Under the old tradition, women's sexuality could lead men astray—women, as with Helen of Troy, could cause the ruin of civilization because of beauty and sex appeal. Women also have power as mothers, in their ability to create life. I think there's an unconscious fear of women's power as sexual beings and mothers, and if you put both of them together it's too much for men to handle.

We like to hope that men are evolving toward an ever-increasing comfort level with powerful women, but this can't happen unless women become comfortable with their own power first. Perhaps envisioning yourself as an extraordinarily potent being is just the inspiration you've been waiting for to assert your maternal sexuality.

The naysayers

When it comes to self-image, we've got more than enough internal demons to deal with. Morphing bodies, shifting priorities, unprecedented demands— our ability to weather these tumultuous changes directly affects our sexual self-confidence. But even if we successfully navigate our way through a maze of self-doubt, there's no predicting what obstacles those around us have stored up to throw in our paths. Approach the subjects of sex and motherhood separately, and there are already plenty of people lined up on their soap boxes ready to pass judgment. But combine the two topics into one real-live human called a "sexual mom" and you'll open a Pandora's box of criticisms.

If the history of attitudes toward women's sexuality has taught us nothing else, it should have taught us not to believe everything we read or hear. Society, science, religion, and your nosy neighbors may seek to define what's "appropriate," but only you know what sex is and should be in your own life. If you can identify the illogic, inconsistency, or misinformation fueling every attack on your sexual expression, you reveal the attack for what it is: not a personal indictment of your motherhood—but a mask for someone else's hang-ups. Each time you deflect a poison arrow aimed at your sex life, your self-esteem gets stronger, and your self-image more clearly defined.

Our survey respondents were not at a loss to identify the myths they encountered when they became mothers:

Myth #1: Sex is for procreation

The "sexual revolution," the invention of birth control, and the self-help movement all trumpet the fact that sex can be engaged in solely for the sheer, body-arching pleasure of it. Yet some people continue to assume that parents are only having sex to reproduce—or alternately, that once you become parents, you forget how to have sex for any other reason!

> Some of my partners seemed really surprised that I was interested in sex at all—one girlfriend told me, "You'd think you'd have learned your lesson after three kids, wouldn't you?"

> Some people that I knew just assumed that I would never have that "normal" young-people sex life again, like, "Too bad you're parents now—no more sex for you guys."

Myth #2: Moms aren't sex objects

One of the biggest shocks to our self-image comes from the realization that many people can't conceive of a woman with a child as a sex object. We become objects for pity, reverence, or dismissal in the eyes of those we used to count on for a little simple sexual validation.

> I was more grounded and sexually confident than ever before, but other people saw me as a "mom." Men quit looking at me in the grocery store when I had the baby with me. They looked at me like they look at my mother. I felt a little disappointed.

> I felt like I was invisible while I was pregnant, and this is true even now when I'm in public with my son. Oddly enough, I still find men flirting with me when my son is NOT with me.

I was in college while raising my son. A lot of the boys there were intimidated by my mom status and I think they found it hard to view me as anything other than someone's mother. I guess it's just the age that college boys are—they can't separate their own mothers from someone who is a mother.

There are many reasons for this sexual invisibility—people assume you're unavailable; they treat you, by extension, as they would treat their own mothers; they don't want to interfere with your family. What you need to remember is: it's no reflection on your actual sex appeal. You may find, as some moms do, that it's a relief to experience a little less unsolicited sexual attention.

I have a lot of male friends and now that I am a mom we are all closer in a new way. They don't seem threatened by me the way they would be by other girls. My friend is always trying out his lines on me and that sort of thing, because I am a woman, but I am also a mother. I think this makes him feel safe around me.

Myth #3: Dads are sexy, but not moms

While many people can't quite wrap their head around the idea of a sexy mom, nobody has too much trouble conceiving of dads as sexy.

I notice that when I walk around with our daughter, I become invisible. When my husband is alone with her, he gets all kinds of attention. Why are men who look like single dads perceived as such chick magnets, yet women who look like they might be single moms cease to exist?

In another example of the double standard, fathers' sex lives are a given—the biggest cause for concern is whether they're getting enough—but mothers' sex lives are not. Mothers who make their sexual needs a priority are deemed oversexed, promiscuous, or even neglectful; fathers who do so are simply exerting their conjugal rights.

When I left my kids' dad, I was considered a "slut" because it was obvious I left for a sexual relationship. Moms who prioritize a sexual life are perceived as irresponsible, selfish, even abusive.

Myth #4: All parents are Ozzie and Harriet

If your family doesn't fit the white-picket-fence ideal, no matter how rock-solid your self-esteem is, it's a challenge to deal with all the inaccurate assumptions you encounter on a daily basis.

> I get so sick of people asking about the baby's dad—I just want to whip out my girlfriend's picture and say "Here's Papa!"

> Being an adoptive mom, I did come across some rude statements by other moms that implied I wasn't a "real" mom.

> Sometimes I feel like wearing a sign when I'm out with my daughter that says "Hey, I am an available, desirable, sex-loving single mom. Date me!" It seems like people just assume I'm taken.

And not every woman who conceives through intercourse with a man appreciates the assumptions that ensue about her sexual orientation.

> I think that people's image of me changed because my hubby was the first man I'd had a long-term relationship with in a while. I'm one of the few in my circle who is openly bi. That gave me a certain sexual cachet. Now, people seem to think that just because I married a man, I'm not bi any more. That's hardly true. I'm just in a straight marriage.

> Lesbians thought I "had to be" hetero! It was a scream since I had been with women nine of the ten previous years before my son was born.

Moms Make Better Lovers

But enough about challenges! Motherhood is also an amazing opportunity to create a richer and more fully integrated self-image. Many women discover that they now feel more whole, and have a greater appreciation for the spirituality inherent in sexuality.

> Being a mom made me feel more complete as a woman. Like two halves coming together. The maternal side and the sexual side com-

bining to form this one magnificent being: Woman. My desire for sex is greater than ever, because I feel that sex is integral to being a complete person, which in turn makes me a much better mom.

I feel even more comfortable with my sexuality because I feel more connected with the whole circle of life. It sounds corny, but it's true.

I feel more sensual. I feel very connected to the earth, I feel very spiritual. This has affected my sexuality immensely.

Others identify motherhood as the wellspring for a newfound power, which translates into more sexual confidence and assertiveness.

I became a sexual goddess in that my beliefs about my body and the power of woman are so much clearer. I became cougar Mama! You know, that "don't fuck with me or my kids or I'll kill you" mentality. For some reason, this made my sexual being more powerful for me and for those around me, male and female.

You may have found that motherhood has inspired a renewed respect and awe for your body. Many biological mothers find that a changed body—weight gain, stretch marks, expanded hips, pendulous breasts, and all—is an unexpected boon to their sexual self-image. Discovering your body's creative capabilities, your strength, and your resilience can yield surprisingly erotic results.

I think I am way more beautiful and powerful and sexy than I used to be. I feel freer sexually. Because we were able to make these amazing creatures through pure fucking! It's great! I appreciate my body so much more, because it has done some wondrous shit, I am just so in awe of it!

The heightened state of awareness from labor hasn't really ended. I'm also really comfortable with my body now, I'm rounder but I feel delicious. I feel sexier than I used to. I stepped beyond a lot of early twenties hang-ups.

And, as this survey respondent discovered, it works both ways. Sex can also bring you back to an awareness of your creative capabilities if you've lost touch with them after motherhood.

I had a special experience with sex after the death of our first child. After the premature birth, hospitalization, and eventual death of our firstborn my body was completely numb. I couldn't feel a thing. It was through sex that I started to regain feeling and the awareness of the physical sensations of my body. Sex reconnected me with my body. Our second baby was born unassisted on the side of the road on the way to the midwife. It was one of the most empowering experiences of my life.

"Moms make better lovers" may sound like bumper sticker hype, but plenty of mothers confirm the slogan, because the qualities that make us good mothers—caring, nurturing, and generosity—are precisely the qualities that make us better lovers.

My children taught me how to truly love someone with total surrender. I learned how to express my love with my partner better than before, which led to better sex.

I didn't know how to love anyone seriously till I had a child. It expanded my humanity, which in turn enhanced my sexuality.

As Susie Bright points out, it's arbitrary to make distinctions between mother love and sexual love:

Maternal love is just one facet of erotic love—because it is the erotic imagination and generosity in our spirit that makes such "maternal" sacrifice and unconditional appreciation possible.[2]

Many women find that motherhood brings them greater sexual maturity. Competitiveness, vanity, and status-seeking are replaced by authenticity and self-expression.

I feel sexier in a different way than I used to. I feel more experienced and whole and less like a seductive teeny-bopper.

I feel more sexually charged, I can tell other people can feel it, too, but it is more mellow and confident than before. I am not as much of a flirt.

Becoming a mom at the age of twenty was an awakening. I had thought of myself as sexual only in the sense of being desirable, or being able to manipulate my sexuality for my physical, monetary, or psychological benefit. Becoming a mother acquainted me with the elemental, sacred aspects of sex that are now a permanent part of my sexual identity. I find my maternal sexuality to be much more appealing to myself and to others. I feel that I am in control.

Becoming a mother teaches you about true intimacy. A child demands intense closeness and offers utter trust; once you discover your own capacity for maternal intimacy, you may find it translates into the realm of sexual intimacy, resulting in a powerful sexuality that is radiantly attractive to your partners.

I soon realized that my new assertiveness (the protective mom factor) made me even more attractive to partners. I have improved with age, and being a mother has only made me softer, harder, more well-rounded, and generally more interesting.

Nothing will improve your self-image quite like bucking the system, asserting your individuality, and reclaiming your right to sex as a woman and a mother. In the process, you challenge others to see you in a different light, and you participate in a cycle of change and growth that we hope will give maternal sexuality the respect it deserves. Here's some parting advice from your fellow moms:

I was told by my family to tone down the Commie Red lipstick and penchant for not wearing slips with see-through dresses. I didn't listen. I see myself as sexier now, like the eternal Earth Mama!

The thing that turned our sex life around was simply my attitude. At some point, I just decided that both I and my husband needed and deserved a good sex life. I started wearing stuff I found sexy. I made exercise a bigger priority because doing it not only actually makes me looks better, but it makes me more confident and unapologetic about my body. I started pushing my body in my husband's way and talking sex up to him even on nights when we couldn't do it. At first, he though it was weird, but I refused to be embarrassed, and he eventually stopped thinking of me as a tired, dried up "soccer mom" and started seeing me as some kind of a sexpot, which is a huge turn-on to him.

Your sexuality has the capacity to fill your life with the same vitality and joy your children do. When you unite the two powerful forces of motherhood and sexuality, you vastly improve your self-image, and you are making a gift to your children. Canadian hip hop artist Michie Mee says it best:

You have to open up as a woman in society. You're not just a hot girl, you're a hot mama and you have to coordinate the two. You cannot put one down; it's a package that doesn't go away, it's an outfit that you do not return. I want to show my son his mom is kooky and sexy. It's more than make-up, hair and clothes—strong sexuality comes from within.[3]

2

Embracing Your
Body Beautiful

Self-esteem is a big business in our culture. Countless books, magazine articles, and inspirational tapes encourage one and all to banish any nagging sense of inadequacy by standing before the mirror and proclaiming, "I'm swell just the way I am." Let us confess upfront that we approach this chapter with some trepidation, well aware that we're not equipped to compete with the best snake-oil salespeople of our generation. We're all too conscious of the fact that affirmations are only skin deep, that our grip on our personal self-esteem is tenuous at best, and that we can't bully you, esteemed reader, into self-confidence. But we are also genuinely angry at how many unjust and unnecessary obstacles block women's access to sexual self-esteem. All those pocket-sized affirmation books are products of the same popular culture that fuels our sexual anxiety with misinformation and mystification. You can't shrug off a sexual inferiority complex by clicking your heels together three times, repeating: "There's no one as sexy as me." But you can distract yourself from your insecurities—pay no attention to the man behind the curtain! Curiosity can be your key to a whole new realm of sexual empowerment. When you stop scrutinizing how you measure up and start exploring your own unique sexuality, you've taken the first step toward a flourishing self-esteem.

Cultivating Positive Body Image

For most women, sexual self-esteem is inextricably entwined with body image—if you feel unattractive, you feel undesirable, and tend to limit your sexual interactions. Conversely, if you feel comfortable in your body, you're more likely to feel deserving of sexual satisfaction, and therefore even more likely to get it. Nothing is quite as sexually appealing as simple self-assurance.

What stands in your way
For women in particular, learning to accept our bodies as they are is a life-long battle. We all know that media depictions of what's "beautiful" or "sexy" are ludicrously limited, yet it's hard to shake the sense that we'd be a whole lot happier if we could just bridge the gap between our own appearance and the fantasy ideal. The media is only part of the problem—our inability to stay in the here and now is another; we tend to postpone appreciating our bodies until that unspecified future point when we'll have attained sufficient perfection to allow ourselves to stop and smell the roses. Even if we move in circles where a wider range of body types is appreciated, nearly every one of us sees something to envy in somebody else's appearance, or something that needs improvement in our own.

To a certain extent, our obsession with improving our bodies reflects a yearning for some manageable sphere of influence; if we can't exert our wills over the body politic, we can at least bring our own bodies into line. After all, despite expanded professional opportunities, fundamental social inequities haven't budged—women still have less earning power than men, and mothers still juggle more than their fair share of responsibility for child care, housework, and child support. No wonder some of us turn to gyms, plastic surgeons, and diet docs to experience a sense of control.

The problem is that when your body is a work in progress, it's hard to find the time amidst all that shaving, exfoliating, toning, and slimming simply to enjoy being in it. A 1998 *Glamour* magazine poll of 27,000 women found that over half the respondents were dissatisfied with their bodies, and that 40% spent more than one-third of their time trying to control their diets. As a result, more respondents said they would rather lose weight than spend a romantic evening with someone they really liked![1]

We all fight the tendency to scapegoat our bodies, and some women face even greater challenges than others. Survivors of child sexual abuse or sexual assault often struggle with negative body image, either feeling detached from, betrayed by, or ashamed of their bodies. Eating disorders are more common in abuse survivors. Even those of us fortunate enough not to face the devastating disempowerment of sexual assault contend with a lesser, low-grade disempowerment: the ongoing commodification of women's bodies.

Why do women fret more about how we look than how we feel? Because we are judged more on how we look than how we feel. Standards of beauty may come and go, but the bottom line never wavers: looks are a woman's ticket to validation and power. Although women tend to be each other's (and our own) harshest critics, our point of reference is always the male gaze. Even the staunchest feminist man inherits the entitlement to judge a woman's appearance, and even the staunchest feminist woman inherits the justifiable anxiety that he will flex his birthright at a moment's notice. If you don't believe this is so, have a lesbian affair, and watch how your body image blooms, how your belly relaxes, how an extra five pounds here or there recedes in importance. We're not suggesting that lesbians don't care about physical attractiveness, just that aesthetic standards become a lot more inclusive once you detour away from mainstream consumer culture.

And we're not blaming men; both sexes suffer equally when women's bodies are treated as status symbols. Sadly, the latest development in popular culture is equal-opportunity objectification; instead of expanding our standards of beauty, we're beginning to enforce equally narrow and unattainable standards for women and men alike. Now young boys are mainlining steroids and pumping iron in a quest to cultivate the ripped chest and washboard abs that are fixtures of contemporary advertising. "Body anxiety for all" seems to be the rallying cry of the twenty-first century, to which we encourage you to retort, "Enough is enough!" and step off the treadmill.

Why take action?

We're encouraging you to develop a more positive body image for three reasons: you owe it to yourself, you owe it to your partners, and you owe it to all the young women in your life.

For yourself

Let's start with you. You're probably already well aware that nothing dampens libido more thoroughly than negative body image. One-third of the *Glamour* survey respondents mentioned above reported that "feeling fat" sometimes prevented them from having sex (and an even higher percentage reported

Hot Tips: Your Sex History

We're often too busy worrying about sex, obsessing about sex, or wishing it would just plain go away to take the long view. But reviewing the patterns in your personal sexual history can shed a lot of light on where you'd like to go from here. You'll probably get the most out of this exercise if you write out your answers (and they'll be of great interest to read further on down the road), but even just pondering these questions as you sit in traffic or lie in the tub can be enlightening.

- What were the early messages you received from relatives, teachers, and peers about sex, reproduction, bodies, masturbation, and gender roles?
- What are your earliest memories of sexual feelings? Of sexual experimentation?
- What was your experience of puberty? Adolescence?
- What was your first sexual experience with another person?
- What have been the most positive and most negative sexual experiences of your life?
- What are your most and least favorite things about your body? About your sexual responses?
- If relevant, how has your history of birth control, pregnancy, and childbirth affected your sexuality? If relevant, how has your history of sexual or medical problems affected your sexuality?
- What are your current sexual practices?
- What are your current fantasies?
- What would you like to change about your sex life?
- What do you imagine your sexuality will be like in 10 years? 20 years? etc.

that receiving a verbal compliment was more likely to make them feel good than having sex).[2] The paradox is that nothing can boost your body image and take your mind off "feeling fat" as effectively as enjoyable sex.

Did you ever stop to consider how many of the people you see out in the world—of all sizes, ages, and abilities—are enjoying active sex lives? In fact the chances are good that if you tried to guess which one of your fellow bus passengers was enjoying the most satisfying sex life, you'd be wrong. Sexual chemistry transcends standards of beauty and subverts expectations, but we remain locked into the assumption that sex is for the young, footloose, and fancy-free, largely because we don't receive much evidence to the contrary. As psychologist Lenore Tiefer puts it:

> Cultural messages, whether they are coming from religion or commercialism, are influential in part because they're not counteracted by your own observation. . . . If you stopped to think, you might say to yourself, "I've never seen ordinary people make love. What do they do with a big stomach? How do they undress each other?" The lack of a bridge between people's own experience and the culture serves to depress us about sexuality.[3]

But when you set aside cultural messages, sex can be a simple holiday from the cult of perfection. In their excellent sex enhancement guide, *Let Me Count the Ways,* therapists Marty Klein and Riki Robbins advise that you:

> Experience your body's perfection during sex. Notice how good kissing doesn't require you to lose weight; notice how having more hair or whiter teeth wouldn't make your orgasms any better. In this sense, sex can be a mental vacation from all the self-criticism your body endures.[4]

You can create your own bridge to an authentic sexuality by looking around you for role models of women who exude sensual assurance. Surely you've noticed that plenty of women who don't fit into a size six dress have vigorous self-esteem (and plenty of women who are cover models don't). Despite the cultural fetish for sexy youth, you'll probably find your best role models among women who aren't spring chicks. This book is filled with quotes from women who testify that maturity and motherhood have brought them a deeper self-acceptance and sexual fulfillment than they had known before.

> I was a very thin, nubile woman before having children. After two children I'm a little Rubenesque, but much more comfortable with it. I'm turning forty in a week or so and am relishing my self these days. I still feel very much the sexual woman. And I try to convey this sense to my daughters in a way that makes sense: "Mommies are loving, caring, and sexual beings."

Too many girls grow up feeling inadequate, because they don't match up to the bodies they see on television or movies. It's taken me forty years to realize that I'm beautiful and desireable at my size (currently 315 lbs), and that I've wasted too many of those years trying to alter the way I look, while feeling that I was unappealing to the opposite sex. It's all an illusion. Confidence and attitude are the most attractive qualities any person can possess.

For your partners

All too often, low self-esteem becomes a way not only to punish yourself, but to punish your partner. Women who are feeling dissatisfied with their appearance are liable either to tune out their partner's expressions of affection and appreciation, or to deflect their advances. But if your partner wants to make love to you, he or she really doesn't need to hear about how fat you feel, or that you have to get to the gym first thing in the morning. If you were to pause in that headlong rush to turn off the lights and take a moment just to focus on what it feels like to touch your lover's body, the unselfconscious joys of sexual satisfaction could be closer than you think.

Negative body image makes us unnecessarily threatened by a lover's appreciation for other people or fantasy materials; we automatically see any desirable "other" as a reflection of our own inadequacy. Just because your husband drools over a porn star's long legs doesn't mean yours don't feel pretty darn great wrapped around his back, and just because your girlfriend religiously watches each and every "Xena: Warrior Princess" episode doesn't mean she's going to leave you for a kickboxing vixen. Let go of that pinched fear, that "I'm not good enough," and switch your focus to an examination of all the different people and situations that arouse your own sexual desires. Sexual curiosity is the first step on the road to sexual generosity.

For girls everywhere

Finally, modeling a positive body image is the single best gift you could bequeath the girls and young women in your life. They are growing up in a world where casual female self-deprecation, if not self-denigration, is the name of the game. We ourselves used to work in a women-owned, feminist sex business, where sexual diversity was sincerely honored and celebrated. You might think that this environment would have been an oasis from negative body image, but we still heard regular variations on those age-old junior high refrains: "You look great, did you lose weight?" or "You're so skinny—I hate you!"

Every time your daughter, younger sister, or niece sees you stand in front of the mirror with a furrowed brow or disgusted expression, she's getting the message that a woman's physical appearance is anxiety-inducing. The *Glamour* survey cited above found that 62% of the women who described their own mothers as having had negative body image inherited this sense of dissatisfaction. And girls who are unhappy with their bodies are girls at risk. As historian Joan Jacobs Brumberg puts it:

> As long as they feel so unhappy with their bodies, it is unlikely that they can achieve the sexual agency that they need for complete and successful lives in the contemporary world. Girls who do not feel good about themselves need the affirmation of others, and that need, unfortunately, almost always empowers male desire. In other words, girls who hate their bodies do not make good decisions about partners, or about the kind of sexual activity that is in their best interest. Because they want to be wanted so much, they are susceptible to manipulation, to flattery, even to abuse.[5]

Sure it's hard to silence the negative tapes in your own head, or to break the habit of companionable fretting with other women, but if you can't do it for yourself, try doing it for the next generation of women, who deserve to blossom into Warrior Princesses one and all. Be vigilant, cultivate perspective, and hold on to your sense of humor. Who knows, maybe the next time somebody asks, "You look great, did you lose weight?" you'll be inspired to answer, "Actually I've gained a couple pounds, but I just had a terrific orgasm, which always makes me look good!" And then take a young girl out to lunch and tell her how beautiful, strong, and smart she is.

Hot Tips: Cultivating Self-Esteem

If your self-esteem could use a boost, try a few of these practical suggestions for exploring your relationship to your body and your sexuality:

- Review your assets. Make a list of the qualities you've always admired in yourself (you don't need to limit yourself to the physical). Describe why you appreciate these qualities and whether you think they're sexy.

- Compare and contrast. Make a list of people you find attractive, friends and strangers alike. Can you pinpoint what it is about them that is so appealing? Which of these appealing characteristics conform to the norm, and which don't?
- Define your terms. What does being a sexy woman mean to you? When you feel sexy, what do you look and feel like, and how are you expressing yourself? If you're not sure you've ever felt sexy, what's your fantasy of what this would be like?
- Take your own sex history. Your background (family, religious, and cultural) and relationship history are all formative influences on your sexual identity. Write your own sex history (see Your Sex History sidebar for details) to get a sense of where you've been and where you might like to go.
- Talk about it. Talk to friends and lovers about what comments or situations hinder or help your self-esteem. Swap tips on coping mechanisms. Talk about what's depicted as sexy in movies, TV, ads, and music videos compared to what's been sexy in your own experience.
- Don't talk about it. Declare a moratorium on conversations about body fat, dieting, cellulite, and skin care. Every time you feel yourself on the verge of a self-critical comment, imagine the snappy retort you'd make if anyone criticized someone you love in those terms (it's so much easier to be generous and gallant to our loved ones than ourselves).
- Develop friendships on-line. People rave about the faceless environment of the Internet, which allows them to get to know each other for who they are, not what they look like. You might get to know and appreciate aspects of yourself that you rarely express face-to-face.
- Go to a nude beach. You'll benefit from the healing sensation of sun and air kissing every inch of your skin—along with a powerful reality check about just how many body types are out there.
- Flaunt it. Give yourself permission to invest in your favorite physical attributes. Try a new hairstyle that draws attention to your lovely eyes, clothes that accentuate your shapely derriere, or a manicure that says, "Kiss my hands, please!"
- Indulge yourself. Give your partner a fifteen-minute body massage. Touch in ways that delight or feel good to you (your partner should only give you feedback if he or she is uncomfortable or in pain). What's it like to touch someone purely for your own pleasure?
- Move it. Walk, dance, bicycle, swim, stretch, masturbate. Move your body in whatever ways feel good.

Appreciating Sexual Anatomy

Even if you've got a good attitude about your figure, your sexual self-esteem can suffer if you don't have an equally good attitude about what's between your legs. An astonishingly large number of women lack the basic physiological information that can put them in control of their own sexual satisfaction. As children, too few of us receive accurate information about our genital anatomy; if anything, we're usually taught that girls have a vagina "down there," and that this is the place for babies to come out of. It can be highly disorienting for a girl who's heard not a peep about pleasure, and has been given no language to describe the clitoris and vulva, to discover that it feels good to rub her clitoris. The adult embarrassment or disapproval that ensue if she's "caught" engaging in self-exploration only reinforce the message that genitals are unmentionable at best and shameful at worst.

The willful ignorance that many women pick up during childhood often extends to our sexual responses. All too many of us take a hands-off, romantic attitude toward sexual pleasure; Prince or Princess Charming is supposed to gallop in on a white steed and take care of the mysterious mechanics of sex without our ever needing to say, "a little to the left, please."

As two women who came of age right along with the women's sexual self-help movement, we're convinced that every single woman alive would benefit from sitting down with a hand mirror and taking a long, loving look at her own genitals. For one thing, they are utterly, miraculously beautiful. For another, every woman's labia, vagina, and clitoris are different, and you deserve to know how you're unique and to experiment with the unique stimulation styles that will please you. Finally, every mother owes it to her children to cultivate a healthy comfort with and appreciation of her genitals, as she's bound to communicate her own attitudes to them.

With that lecture out of the way, let us take you on a whirlwind tour from top to bottom of your genital anatomy.

A genital tour

The external female genitals are referred to as the vulva, and consist of the labia, the clitoral glans, the vaginal opening, and the urethral opening. The two long fleshy folds of the outer lips, the labia majora, are composed of fat and erectile tissue, and covered with pubic hair. The most distinctive portion of the vulva tends to be the labia minora, the smooth, hairless inner lips that enclose the urethral and vaginal openings. Labia come in a range of sizes, colors, and shapes, and they are not likely to come as a matched pair. Many women have suffered shame and embarrassment thinking that their labia were deformed or unsightly because one lip hung lower than the other, or because they weren't tucked discreetly inside the vulva. Women simply aren't exposed to much vulva imagery and don't necessarily have any frame of reference (no, Georgia O'Keefe paintings do not count!). If you've ever thought your own or any woman's genitals were ugly or abnormal, we encourage you to check out Betty Dodson's artwork for glorious depictions of the women's genitalia in all their variety.

The labia minora meet in small folds at the top of the vulva, right above the clitoral glans. If you pull back this hood of skin to take a closer look, you may be intrigued to see how much the clitoral glans resembles a miniaturized version of the glans of a penis (sans urethral opening). Small as it is, it's power-packed—the clitoris is made up of some 8,000 nerve fibers, a higher concentration than in any other part of the body (and twice as many as in the penis). The exquisitely sensitive glans sits on top of the short clitoral shaft that runs beneath the skin in the direction of the pubic bone—if you press down on the skin above your clitoris, you can feel the shaft rolling beneath your fingers. The shaft is attached to the two clitoral legs (also called crura), which are about three inches long and extend beneath the labia, arcing like two halves of a wishbone on either side of the vaginal and urethral openings.

The clitoral shaft and legs have far fewer nerve endings than the glans, but are made of spongy erectile tissue that is rich in blood vessels. During sexual arousal, increased blood flow to the vulva engorges the labia as well as the entire clitoral body, which swells and becomes firmer—it's not exactly like a man's erection, but darn close. The reality of women's anatomy is that there's really no such thing as a clitoral versus a vaginal orgasm, because we can't stimulate any part of our genitals without indirectly stimulating the clitoral body. The labia and vagina are sensitive erogenous zones, but while some women can orgasm with general genital stimulation, the majority of women require direct stimulation of the clitoral glans to get over the top. In fact, although Freud's decree that clitoral pleasure was "immature" cast a long shadow over our understanding of women's sexuality during the twentieth century, for thousands of years before that, the clitoris was well-known as the main site of female sexual pleasure. A typical passage from a nineteenth-century marital guide describes the clitoris as an organ that can "stir up lust and give delight in copulation, for without this the fair sex neither desire nuptial embraces nor have pleasure in them."[6]

The urethral opening lies between the clitoris and the vaginal opening. The skin around the opening is rich in nerve endings, and some women find stimulation of this area highly pleasurable. The urethra itself is a slender, short tube that conducts urine out of the bladder. It runs above and parallel to the vagina and is surrounded by spongy erectile tissue, containing paraurethral glands and ducts ("para" means "beside," or "near"). This "urethral sponge" is what's come to be much hyped as the "G-spot." Why a spot? Well, the urethra itself is only one and a half to two inches long, so the urethral sponge isn't very large. The erectile tissue of the urethral sponge swells during sexual arousal, at which point you can feel the G-spot by pressing hard against the front wall of the vagina. Some women find G-spot stimulation highly arousing, and some also find that it can lead to ejaculation of a clear, odorless fluid. Although this fluid is ejaculated through the urethra, it's chemically distinct from urine. All women have a urethral sponge, but only some women ejaculate.

The vaginal opening lies just below the urethral opening. If you have witnessed or experienced vaginal delivery firsthand, you have doubtless developed great respect for the muscular expansiveness of the vagina. Made of muscle and tissue, lined with mucous membrane, the vagina is about four inches long and curves at roughly a forty-five degree angle up toward the cervix, the neck of that other amazingly muscular organ, the uterus. While the vagina is often compared to a tunnel or hole, the vaginal walls rest companionably against each other most of the time, only to expand outward upon sexual arousal (or during childbirth).

Reach just inside your vaginal opening, and you'll feel a slightly ridged surface, especially along the front wall just behind the pubic bone, where the urethral sponge protrudes. The outer third of the vagina, which contains more nerve endings than the inner two-thirds, can be quite responsive to touch. The inner two-thirds of the vaginal walls are smoother and more responsive to pressure than touch.

The perineum is the small stretch of skin between the vaginal opening and the anus, and is an erogenous zone in its own right. Another body of erectile tissue, referred to as the perineal sponge, lies between the back wall of the vagina and the rectum, and probably contributes to pleasurable sensation during both vaginal and anal penetration. During vaginal labor, the perineum may tear, or the laboring woman may be given an episiotomy, a surgical cut through the skin of the perineum designed to reduce the risk of further tearing during delivery. Since the perineum is the site of many nerves and crisscrossing pelvic floor muscles, an episiotomy can result in some loss of sexual sensation, though many women find that a tear or episiotomy has no long-term effects on their genital sensitivity.

Hot Tips: Love Your Genitals

You may be the most self-assured, body-loving, bold-faced nudist in town, but if you don't have a genuine appreciation for your own genitals, your sex life will suffer. Have you ever felt a flicker of anxiety as a lover's mouth headed between your legs? Have you ever worried, "Does he think I look/smell/taste okay?" or "Isn't she getting bored down there?" Then it's time for a crash course in vulva love.

- Draw a picture of your labia. Get out the hand mirror, and sketch what you see. Your efforts to capture the artful nature of every fold could arouse a new appreciation for your intimate architecture.
- Tour your genitals. Take a manual tour, touching and caressing every inch of your vulva, labia, and clitoris. Consider this an information-gathering expedition, rather than an effort to arouse. Just let yourself experience the different types of skin and sensation.
- Have a taste. Forget about those fish jokes—a healthy vagina smells and tastes just dandy, but you're going to have a hard time believing this unless you test it for yourself. Check how your natural secretions change in texture and taste throughout your menstrual cycle. (If your vagina does veer too far from its sweet, tangy norm, there's probably a bacterial imbalance you'll need to address.)
- Rock around the clock. Explore your vagina to discover your own personal pleasure spots. Envision your vagina as a clock face, and your fingers as the hands of the clock; travel round the clock, pressing your fingers firmly into the vaginal walls and noting where you're extra sensitive. Time will fly.

The anus is also loaded with nerve endings, which is why anal stimulation can be just as arousing as genital stimulation. While anal play carries a taboo as being somehow "dirty" or "dangerous," it's a natural, safe form of eroticism. Many folks of all sexualities enjoy the pleasurable pressure of anal penetration. If you're going to explore this form of eroticism, you should practice relaxing your anal sphincter muscles; the external sphincter muscle is under voluntary control, but the internal sphincter is involuntary and will tighten if you rush or force penetration, with painful results. Any anal penetration, whether with a pinkie or a penis, should always be accompanied by a generous application of lubricant, since the rectum doesn't self-lubricate, and rectal tissue is much more delicate than vaginal tissue.

Pelvic muscles

Pelvic muscles play a major role in a woman's experience of sexual pleasure—and in her overall health. The pelvic muscles lie about an inch beneath your pelvic floor and are attached like a sling to your pubic bone at one end and your tailbone or coccyx at the other—that's why they're also referred to as the pubococcygeus muscle or "PC" muscle. The singular term, "PC muscle," actually refers to a group of interconnected, multi-layered muscles that support the entire pelvic floor and form a figure eight encircling the vagina, urethra, and rectum in women, and the base of the penis and rectum in men.

Pelvic muscles play a key role in sexual sensation—they're loaded with nerve endings and contract involuntarily during orgasm. Learning to control these muscles voluntarily not only has numerous health benefits, it heightens sexual responsiveness. If your pelvic muscles are well-toned, you'll have increased genital sensation, greater vaginal lubrication, and more powerful orgasms.

The importance of pelvic muscle control is known and taught around the world—belly dancing, Hula, and much African dance depend on it. But true to form, in America we trace our information on pelvic muscles exercises back to a medical authority. Gynecologist Arnold Kegel devised a simple series of exercises in the forties to treat urinary incontinence, and these exercises have since become known as "Kegels." If you're a biological mother, these are all too familiar to you, as you'll have been encouraged to do Kegels both in preparation for labor and to speed recovery postpartum. Kegels entail repetitive tightening and relaxing of the pelvic muscles—either in a sequence of quick squeezes, or in a slower pulling up and bearing down. The easiest way to identify the pelvic muscles is to stop and start the flow of urine; the muscles you use to do so are the pelvic muscles.

Sure, you can do Kegels at any time, but these are exercises that beg to be incorporated with sexual activities. For one thing, it's particularly helpful to have a penis or dildo inside your vagina as a resistive device while exercising. For another, since Kegels increase sensation in, and blood flow to, the genitals, they can enhance any sexual encounter. You can heighten arousal by coordinating Kegels with breathing—inhaling as you contract, and exhaling as you relax—or with pelvic rocking.

What about sexual response?

We're not going to give you any song and dance about the sexual response cycle, largely because throughout this book we encourage you to get to know your own body and to identify your unique sexual responses and preferences. Sure, there are certain constants of physiological response common to all individuals: the increased blood flow, genital swelling, and muscular tension of arousal, and the discharging of this tension through the muscular contractions of orgasm. But there's a wide range of subjective experience that the monolithic model of one "sexual response cycle" is woefully inadequate to express. If you are someone who has never reached, or doesn't reliably reach, orgasm we refer you to the Resources section for some recommended reading. If you are someone who does reliably orgasm, we doubt the experience would be enhanced for you by learning that Masters and Johnson clocked orgasmic contractions as occurring every eight-tenths of a second.

Sexual self-knowledge is not a one-time journey of discovery in which you map out your personal terrain once and for all. In fact, our experience of sexual response is ever-evolving over the course of a lifetime, and why should it be otherwise? Our physical bodies change over time, and our relationship to our bodies changes over time—it's no more likely that the pattern of sexual response we develop in adolescence will remain relevant throughout our adulthood than that our adolescent relationship style will. If you're able to put aside societal messages about what's sexually "normal" and simply listen to your own body's responses, you'll be able to reap the greatest amount of sexual pleasure out of your evolving experience.

Attitudes about Sexual Pleasure

Wouldn't it be great if, instead of talking with other moms at the playground about our kids' latest accomplishments, we could swap stories about our own latest erotic adventures? You gasp! But think about it—we share intimate details about our children's biological functions with near strangers; what prevents us from talking about our own urges and desires with such candor? Unfortunately, we live in a society where such sexual frankness is discouraged—a profound loss for mothers considering how much we could learn from each other about loving our bodies, keeping the flame alive, and exploring our fantasies.

Instead, we're left to our own devices to decipher the mixed messages we receive about sexuality. Our society places great value on the family and sex-for-procreation, yet we receive no reality-based sex education or relationship training, so we muddle our way through our first sexual and emotional experiences, risking embarrassment and failure. We slowly gain confidence and expertise, but may be hounded throughout our lives by the questions, "Am I good enough?" or "Is what I'm doing normal?" As we grow more adventurous we confront one label after another: If we enjoy having sex often, we're promiscuous. If we enjoy alternatives to intercourse, we're kinky. If we are taking a break from partner sex, we're frigid. We receive so many conflicting messages from parents, friends, church, medical professionals, magazine articles, and lovers about what, when, where, how and why (or why not) to have sex that it's easy to forget why we have it in the first place: because it feels good and because it's good for us.

After all, we share a Victorian heritage that values self-control over self-expression, and considers abstinence a virtue. Women in particular have internalized the message that it's possible to have "too much pleasure," and that the pursuit of pleasure is necessarily a selfish act. As mothers we're subjected to specific scripts that play right into this philosophy, inhibiting intimacy and curbing sexual expression. Somehow, "Children come first, our needs come second" means that sex winds up as the last thing on our agenda. The desire to be good parental role models can lead us to limit or closet our own sexual behavior out of fear that we'll be setting some sort of bad example.

It takes confidence and self-awareness to reject these messages and to proudly embrace your sexuality. It also takes self-acceptance. If you approach the cultivation of self-esteem as one more "should" on your list of "ways to be a better person," you're setting yourself up for failure. Nurturing sexual self-esteem is an ongoing process, and you're bound to hit some bumps in the road. When you're feeling negative about yourself, your body, or your sexuality, try to uncover what's fueling these feelings and keep in mind that they'll pass. After all, every time you assert your right to be sexual—whether you're buying a tight new dress that highlights your womanly figure or hiring a babysitter so you can enjoy a sensuous afternoon masturbating—you'll reap the undeniable rewards.

3

Good Sex
Starts with You

We'd be happy to put our cards on the table and tell you just what we think about masturbation . . . but then we'd have to take our hands out from under the sheets! Few topics inspire our personal gratitude or stimulate our inner cheerleaders to boundless enthusiasm as much as masturbation. Our frustration that this beloved pastime doesn't receive the public acceptance it so richly deserves inspired us to inaugurate the first National Masturbation Month, an annual celebration of the fine art of self-loving sponsored by our alma mater, San Francisco's Good Vibrations.

What's to celebrate? So many things: masturbation is fun, it's easy, it's relaxing, it's pleasurable, and it's available to individuals of all ages, sex styles, and abilities. Masturbation is a crucial component of any satisfying sex life, and an unparalleled way to honor and express your sexuality from cradle to grave.

Why Do It?

If you've never masturbated, you may not be sure how you'd go about it. Take heart—there are some excellent guidebooks written especially for women that offer detailed instructions and encouragement (look in the Resources section for information on Lonnie Barbach's *For Yourself* and Betty Dodson's *Sex For One*). Even if you enjoy masturbation, you may not have thought much about why it's such a delightful form of sexual expression. Read our list of just a few of masturbation's many benefits, and you may develop new insights and ideas.

It boosts your sexual energy

When your time, energy, and personal space are limited, your libido usually disappears. It's not that you wouldn't like to feel the pulsing, tingling thrill of good old-fashioned arousal, it's just that you can't exactly be bothered to pursue it. But when it comes to sex, nothing succeeds like excess. The more sexual pleasure you experience, the more you're motivated to have. Masturbation can be a great way to jump-start your stalled sex drive, because it's unconstrained. You don't have to coordinate desire with a partner, or contend with performance anxiety; you simply go at your own pace and focus on what feels good.

> My satisfaction comes from my willingness to take good care of my own sexual needs rather than let my desires fall by the wayside.

It teaches you about your own responses

We aren't born knowing what pleases us sexually, and chances are you've gotten to a relatively ripe age without knowing every possible quirk of your sexual responses. Masturbation is a brilliant way to explore your genital anatomy and sensual preferences. Many girls and women have their first orgasms, multiple orgasms, or G-spot orgasms from masturbation. Unrestricted by the "rules" and expectations that plague partner sex, you can experiment with intensifying your own arousal through techniques such as deep breathing, flexing and releasing your pelvic muscles, moving your hips, stopping and starting stimulation, building tension. Think of all the time you've probably put into activities like perfecting your cheesecake recipe, or coming up with a thoughtful handmade holiday craft—don't you deserve to put at least that much time into discovering just how much sexual pleasure you're capable of having?

> I used to masturbate in the same way, always getting very rigid, taking short breaths and cramping up. A friend told me to try taking deep breaths while approaching orgasm, and I was shocked at a) how hard it was to give up my tried-and-true method and b) how strongly I felt that orgasm to the tips of my toes when I did breathe into it!

It allows you to fantasize freely

Exploring your fantasies during partner sex may seem awkward if you believe that your attention should be focused on the matter at hand. Masturbation is a powerful tool for mental, as well as physical, self-exploration. On your own, with nobody else present to inhibit or censor you, you can let your fancy wander. Determining what thoughts, feelings, or images stimulate your desire is just as crucial to a fulfilling sex life as determining what kind of touch stimulates your clitoris. Masturbation allows you to explore both in tandem.

It feels good

If masturbation doesn't feel good to you, we suggest you review the following information on the masturbation taboo. Many of us have been raised to believe that masturbation is an immature, self-polluting, inappropriate form of behavior, and it can be difficult to shove these negative messages aside long enough to access the pure and simple pleasure of touching yourself. Trust us, you did it as a tiny baby, and you can do it again.

It's good for you

We bet you don't exercise as much as you feel you should. And even though you clip all those nutritious recipes, we doubt you're adhering to the healthy diet you resolve to follow every January 1. Well take heart, masturbation is an activity that doesn't force you to choose between looking good and feeling good. Masturbation is a form of exercise: it increases blood and oxygen flow to your genitals, strengthens your pelvic muscles, and serves as a mild cardiovascular workout (ankle weights are optional). Like all exercise, it relieves stress, releases endorphins, and promotes a general sense of health and well-being.

It's creative

Masturbation has the power to renew, refresh, invigorate, and heal largely because it's a creative act. As parents, we get so little private time in which to gather our thoughts and marshal our resources that we tend to compensate by seeking refreshment through consumption: we take our breaks by having a cigarette, drinking a latte, eating some chocolate, or shopping for treats. But masturbation isn't about consumption; it's about creation. It blends the soul-satisfying joys of privacy and erotic self-expression, leaving you more energized and exhilarated after the fact than when you started.

Since I'm not partnered, I masturbate whenever it doesn't interfere with child raising—like when my son is watching TV. It gives me some crucial time all to myself.

You can share it with a loved one
If the above reasons sound just a wee bit too self-serving to you, keep in mind that all the information you glean about your sexual preferences, responses, and stamina will be of great interest to your partners. One of the all-time best ways to learn how you and a partner can please each other is to masturbate together.

We masturbate, alone and together, more often than we have intercourse. Sometimes we just want to come. Enjoying my own body has really helped me to enjoy my partner's body also.

Hot Tips: Masturbation Styles

- with water: bathtub faucets, shower massagers, hot tub jets
- with vibrators: clitoral, insertable, hands-free, waterproof
- with dildos: anal plugs, vaginal dildos, produce, strap-ons
- with oil: anoint your erogenous zones and be a sacred priestess of love
- on the sly: pressed up against the washing machine, riding a motorcycle, climbing a pole, rubbing against the seam of your tightest jeans
- quietly: get under the covers and breath softly
- loudly: breath deeply, moan, don't hold back
- with Kegels: contracting and releasing your pelvic muscles will enhance arousal
- with a lover: I'll do you if you do me *any way you want!*

History of a Taboo

By now you may be thinking, "Gosh, if masturbation's so swell, why does everybody treat it like one great big sniggering joke?" Unfortunately, we've inherited a grab bag of religious and cultural beliefs about masturbation that are relentlessly negative. In the Western World, our attitudes about sexuality are rooted in Judeo-Christian and Greek philosophy, and grafted onto the medical "wisdom" of the day. Here's a brief survey of masturbation's checkered career.

It ain't necessarily so

The Old Testament writers emphasized procreative sex as the only acceptable form of sexual expression for the ancient Israelites, both because population growth was literally their means of expanding social and political power, and because the Israelites used dietary and sexual prohibitions to symbolically distinguish themselves from surrounding cultures (in which cult prostitution and homosexuality were common). Many modern-day assumptions about sexual morality derive from biblical stories that have been taken out of context, or in some cases completely misinterpreted: The story of Onan, who "spilled his seed upon the ground" and was struck dead for this sin, is popularly believed to be a story about masturbation (which explains the derivation of the word "Onanism"). In fact, it's a story about how he chose the withdrawal method of birth control when tradition dictated that he should impregnate his dead brother's widow. Although religious teachings may leave you with the vague sense that "the Bible says masturbation is wrong," the Bible actually has nothing to say on the subject.

Woodsman, spare that seed!

So where does Greek philosophy come in? As far back as the fourth century BC, Aristotle was writing that semen is a precious, finite fluid, and that "spending" this valuable substance would sap a man's strength. The idea that semen is an almost magically potent fluid that shouldn't be squandered is found around the world. Chinese Taoist philosophy holds that women's Yin energy is inexhaustible, but that male Yang energy is a river that can all too easily run dry (hence Taoist sexual techniques for men focus on achieving orgasm without ejaculation).

This economic metaphor was taken to new extremes in the mid-nineteenth century, when Samuel Tissot's 1758 tract, *Onanism: Treatise on the Diseases Produced by Masturbation,* was first published in English. Tissot railed against the debilitating affects of masturbation, which he felt leeched women and men alike of vital life force. Although women clearly didn't have to worry about wasting a limited allotment of semen, masturbation nonetheless rendered them vulnerable to losing their minds and being driven to a uterine fury "which deprives them at once of modesty and reason and puts them on the level of the lewdest brutes, until a despairing death snatches them away from pain and infamy."[1]

"The most degrading act that a human being can commit"[2]
Throughout the nineteenth century, masturbation was viewed as a dangerous activity resulting in all manner of ill health, from acne to dementia. Basically, any disease of unknown origin was blamed on "the solitary vice," and all the scare stories you've ever heard about masturbation's terrible side effects (hairy palms, blindness, etc.) probably date back to this era. An entire industry grew up around preventing young boys and girls from playing with themselves. Bondage belts, mittens, and dire injunctions to keep hands outside the covers were the milder forms of treatment. Spiked penile rings (designed to inhibit erections) and clitoridectomy were among the more horrifying treatments; the last clitoridectomy in the US intended to "cure" masturbation was perpetrated on a five-year-old in 1948.[3]

Damned with faint praise
By the twentieth century, masturbation had lost its notoriety as a life-threatening hobby. Exposed to the ideas of Sigmund Freud and sexologist Havelock Ellis, Americans gleaned the message that it was potentially more dangerous to suppress sexual desires than to express them. Freud's theories that all humans pass through a variety of stages on the road to sexual maturity (oral, anal, narcissistic) simultaneously removed masturbation from the category of unnatural activities and deposited it neatly in the category of immature activities. Despite the fact that every sex researcher from Kinsey on has hammered home the fact that the vast majority of people masturbate, and despite the fact that sex educators practically get down on their knees and plead with one and all to explore its many benefits, to this day countless people still consider masturbation to be, at best, a childish activity.

The Love of a Lifetime

Even if you've studied up on the history of the taboo, you may remain somewhat guilt-ridden about masturbating. Most folks who are embarrassed, touchy, or sheepish about masturbating are under the thrall of the most tenacious stereotype of all: the idea that masturbation isn't really sex!

Maybe you think that sex doesn't count as sex unless two people are present. Maybe you think masturbation is only acceptable if you're doing field work in order to report your findings back to your lover. Maybe you think it's somewhat shameful to touch your very own genitals just for the fun of it, to stroke your very own skin and admire how smooth and silky it feels beneath your fingers. Please make every effort to address these feelings head on, and, in the immortal words of one of Cathy's favorite soap opera characters, "Feel it, deal with it, get over it!"[4]

If you are feeling sexual excitement, stimulating your genitals, arousing your senses, and striving for the delicious release of orgasm—you are having sex. It doesn't matter if there's nobody, one lover, two lovers, or a crowd of spectators in the room with you (the crowd of spectators is an excellent fantasy enhancer). Take a tip from your young children and let yourself marvel and delight in how interesting, amazing, and stimulating your body truly is. Masturbation is a lifelong pleasure, and you shouldn't deny yourself this pleasure at any age. You'll masturbate as a baby, as a teenager, as an adult, as a gorgeous old woman. Your partner sex life will have its ups and downs, and lovers will come and go. Through it all, masturbation keeps you in touch with your own innate eroticism. Enjoy.

4

Sometimes You're Hot and Sometimes You're Not

You can be intimately well-acquainted with your sexual anatomy and responses, utterly comfortable with your body, and an exquisitely skilled communicator, but if you don't have desire, you won't want to have sex. Desire is the alchemist's stone that transforms the raw matter of reproductive biology into the glittering gold of sexual expression (and inspires lyrical language in even the most pragmatic sex writers!). Throughout this book, we use terms such as "sex drive" or "libido" to describe a basic physiological ready-willing-and-ableness, but we use the term "desire" to point to the ineffable spark of eroticism that makes sex so—well—desirable. Desire is the essential component to a satisfying sexuality, yet it can be so unpredictable and complicated. And well it should be! Desire brings into play your anatomy and biochemistry, certainly, but also your memories, fantasies, life experience, cultural beliefs—everything that makes you the unpredictable and complicated woman that you are. In this chapter, we'll look at the various forces influencing desire and suggest ways to identify and appreciate your own unique patterns.

Desire and Culture

Your expectations and understanding of sexual desire are inevitably shaped by the world around you. Sure, sexual impulses are perfectly "natural," but the way we think and feel about them is profoundly influenced by culture.

The more things change . . .

Don't be surprised if you experience a certain amount of ambivalence about exploring your own sexual yearnings. After all, simply by asserting your entitlement to sexual desire, you are challenging literally thousands of years of cultural conditioning. You're familiar with the expression, "The more things change, the more they stay the same"? For thousands of years, cultural attitudes around female desire have see-sawed between "women are insatiable, lusty devils whose sexual appetites must be controlled" and "women are innocent, chaste angels who must be protected from men's sexual appetites." In trying to control the means of reproduction, male-dominated societies down through the ages have established restrictions on women's bodies—including the highly effective restriction of telling women what is appropriate for them to think or feel about sex. And so twenty-first-century women still grow up believing that "men want sex, women want romance" or that "women have lower sex drives than men." Just because you might be able to find examples in your own life that seem to support these truisms doesn't mean that they reflect innate, biological truths. The last thing a fish is likely to notice is water, and we all—women and men alike—are swimming in the same sea of cultural assumptions and expectations. Furthermore, sex is a much riskier proposition for women than for men. As one primatologist points out:

> It seems premature to attribute the relative lack of female interest in sexual variety to women's biological nature alone in the face of overwhelming evidence that women are consistently beaten for promiscuity and adultery. If female sexuality is muted compared to that of men, then why must men the world over go to extreme lengths to control and contain it?[1]

Consider what a woman risks by expressing herself sexually: Heterosexual women risk pregnancy and disease when they engage in intercourse. Women of all sexualities risk being dismissed or attacked as "sluts," "nymphomaniacs," or "bad mothers" if they so much as display interest in, let alone pursue, sexual pleasure. Women make up the overwhelming majority of sexual assault victims. Given this social backdrop, it's a testament to the power and tenacity of women's desire that so many of us find a way to embrace, enact, and celebrate our eroticism.

Medical models

The first generation of modern sex therapists and educators in the sixties, heirs to the work of Alfred Kinsey and Masters and Johnson, generally believed that inhibition and ignorance were the only impediments to a satisfying sex life. Kinsey's documentation of the varieties of sexual behavior expanded the definitions of sexual "normalcy," while Masters and Johnson's research on the physiology of sexual response gave a clinical stamp of approval to orgasms for both women and men. In the first flush of the new dawn of sexology, many therapists were understandably confident that given accurate information about sexual anatomy and response, a few sensate focus exercises, and encouragement that sex is "normal" and "healthy," any individual could walk off into the sunset of orgasmic fulfillment. Indeed many could and still do—as former vibrator saleswomen, we can certainly vouch for the power of simple information ("Most women need clitoral stimulation to reach orgasm") and encouragement ("There's nothing wrong with you if you need clitoral stimulation to reach orgasm") to transform an individual's experience of sex.

However, man can't live by bread alone, and woman can't experience sexual pleasure from clitoral stimulation alone. If sexual satisfaction were simply a matter of locating the right buttons to twiddle, sex wouldn't capture our imagination, tug at our heartstrings, and stimulate our mind the way it does. And in fact, basic anatomical information is not enough to guarantee sexual pleasure for all. People need to desire sex to enjoy having sex. By the late seventies, sex therapists had to expand their nuts-and-bolts approach to include issues of desire. Sex therapist Helen Singer Kaplan amended the sexual response cycle proposed by Masters and Johnson (excitement, plateau, orgasm, and resolution) to include desire as a necessary prerequisite to excitement and orgasm, and her model (desire, excitement, orgasm) has been widely followed ever since.

Twenty years ago, sex professionals broke away from the notion that sex is solely a matter of biological responses and acknowledged the power and primacy of desire. Yet in recent years the pendulum has swung back toward physiology as the be-all and end-all of sexual satisfaction, taking desire right along with it. The concept of desire has been medicalized to such an extent that a list of so-called "desire disorders" are now clinically categorized as "sexual dysfunctions" in the DSM (the Diagnostic and Statistical Manual of Mental Disorders). Therefore, if you, dear reader, are experiencing difficulty getting aroused or reaching orgasm, or have sexual urges less often than is decreed "normal," you have a medically treatable condition. And you better believe that drug companies are lining up to treat you with Viagra-style products that work to increase blood flow to the genitals or to increase vaginal lubrication. In 1999, The Journal of the American Medical Association published a study reporting that 43% of American women experience sexual dysfunction ("lack of interest in sex" being most commonly reported). Both the authors of this study just happened to be paid consultants to Pfizer, the company raking in the big bucks on Viagra.[2]

So how did desire become a medically treated condition? Probably because of our culture's deep-seated discomfort with sex. Sure, popular magazines, advice columns, and TV shows are filled with tips on how to make your sex life bigger, harder, hotter, and simultaneously better than, but as normal as, that of the folks next door. But the all-American preference is always for quick-fix solutions at the expense of any thoughtful, potentially discomfiting examination of what actually turns us on and why. Ultimately, it takes less time to design ways to keep penises erect and vaginas supple and well-lubed than to reevaluate the social forces that conspire against authentic expressions of eroticism. Instead, we group sexual desire and sexual function together as engineering problems that can be resolved with mechanical solutions.

The fact is desire involves so much more than physical responsiveness. Your genitals can be displaying every sign of physical arousal, but that doesn't mean you're interested in sex any more than a man who gets an erection during a rectal exam is interested in getting down with his doctor on the exam table. Throughout this book, we discuss ways to enhance your physical responses—blood flow to the genitals is indeed conducive to arousal, and ample lubrication is indeed essential to pleasurable penetration. But, and this is a big but, you can't separate your genitals from the rest of your body and mind—and why would you want to?

A 1994 study by University of Amsterdam psychologist Ellen T. M. Laan is revealing in its distinction between physiological and subjective experiences of arousal. She showed the forty-seven women in her study group two different explicit videos—one a generic mainstream porn video, and the other a video by feminist filmmaker Candida Royalle, which depicted a sexual encounter that the actress clearly enjoyed. The women's physiological responses to both videos were the same—increased genital blood flow and lubrication—but they reported finding the Candida Royalle video highly arousing and the mainstream video an annoying turn-off. In other words, the video they enjoyed watching boosted their desire, and the video they didn't enjoy watching did not, despite their knee-jerk physiological responses. Context is everything. Of course the study didn't look at the ways in which women might be culturally conditioned to enjoy—or be willing to admit enjoying—only certain kinds of erotic imagery. Indeed, there are plenty of women who might report as much arousal from hardcore "wall-to-wall" porn as men—but that's a separate issue. The issue for this researcher boils down to one practical point: just because a woman is wet doesn't mean she's ready.[3] We're willing to bet you've had experience with this phenomenon yourself.

The trouble with the medical model of desire and arousal is that it establishes penis/vagina intercourse as the only acceptable game in town and establishes folks with firm, youthful, well-oiled genitals as the only acceptable players. This is why many sex educators and therapists are tearing their hair out over Viagra. Sex educators used to be able to counsel people that growing older meant growing wiser, that slower responses or less reliable erections could open up a whole new world of erotic experimentation in which the goal shifted from pure performance to pure pleasure. It's difficult for the voices of those challenging the cult of intercourse to be heard over the din of all that erection construction.

Don't get us wrong: penetration is nifty. And truth be told, as women who came of age in the seventies, we have friendly feelings toward recreational drugs and would even be curious to try Viagra once or twice. Certainly, if age and disease cause vascular problems that impede genital arousal, we'd never argue with a person's right to explore medical treatment. But an adult's experience of sex is supposed to evolve over the years. That's the beauty of it. As you age, your physical abilities change—maybe they even deteriorate in some ways—but your emotional life gains depth, your imagination becomes bolder, your sense of self becomes stronger, and you have the capacity to access and enact sexual desires that the three-minute-orgasm contingent would, at the very least, never have time for. How's a grown woman supposed to sustain her sexual appetite over a lifetime if dreary, wham-bam adolescent sexual intercourse is the only item on the menu for literally decades!? The "intercourse or bust" model of sexual desire doesn't only exclude same-sex couples, it excludes everyone who enjoys a richer, more varied palette of sensual pleasures.

As you make your own way through your sexual lifetime, cultural attitudes about what it means to be a woman and a mother are bound to influence, or even inhibit, how you express yourself sexually. Let your own experience be your teacher, let your own desires be your guide, and keep in mind that both of these will be in constant flux throughout your life. Sometimes you'll crave a three-minute orgasm, sometimes you'll orchestrate a three-hour sensual symphony, and sometimes you'll want no genital activity at all. What you yearn for today won't necessarily be what you yearn for tomorrow, but each and every one of your desires has something to teach you about who you are and who you're becoming.

Desire and Your Body

The current emphasis on the physiology of desire also reflects a recent surge of research into the role hormones play on human behavior. Hormones are substances produced in the tissues of one part of the body that travel to other parts of the body and stimulate activity there. (For instance, estrogen produced by the ovaries during the first half of your menstrual cycle prompts your cervix to produce mucus and your uterine lining to plump up.) The hormones that play a big role in a woman's reproductive life—estrogen, testosterone, progesterone, oxytocin, prolactin—also have an impact on her sexual experiences. All these hormones except progesterone are present in both men and women; however women have up to ten times as much estrogen as men during their reproductive years, and men have over ten times as much testosterone as women. Therefore, when research is done on the links between estrogen, testosterone, and libido, these studies are often interpreted to explain desire differences between women and men.

Even if you've read very little on the subject, you've almost certainly picked up the idea that testosterone is the hormone of lust and aggression. Some researchers believe that testosterone levels are the primary determinant of how libidinous you will be and distinguish between "low T" and "high T" individuals. According to this model, your biochemistry—specifically your body's testosterone levels—predisposes you to have either a low or a high sex drive. Since men, by definition, have higher levels of testosterone than women, presto, there's your explanation for the "fact" that "women have lower sex drives than men."

But perhaps you've also picked up the idea that estrogen has a role to play in women's libido. Or maybe you've noticed a fairly regular rise and fall in your own interest in sex over the course of your menstrual cycle. There are studies that suggest that—all other factors being equal—women tend to experience an increase in libido right before ovulation when their estrogen levels are highest. In fact there's some evidence that, to the extent that testosterone boosts libido in women, this is only because proteins that would normally bind to and interfere with estrogen bind to testosterone instead, thereby freeing estrogen to go about its inspirational business.[4] It's helpful to bear in mind that hormone research is in its infancy; hormones were isolated less than one hundred years ago, and scientific understanding of how they operate is still evolving, with previous theories overturned on a regular basis.

Throughout this book, we'll pay all due respect to the powerful influence hormonal fluctuations can have on your state of mind, emotions, body, and sex life. In fact, we'd encourage you to pay attention to the ways in which your own levels of energy and desire may rise and fall cyclically. Hormones fluctuate in daily, monthly, seasonal, and situational cycles that researchers are only beginning to identify—for instance, studies of testosterone levels in men show that they peak in the morning, dip in the late afternoon, increase in the autumn, and decrease during times of stress. Certainly women are familiar with the impact of hormones during physiological life changes such as puberty, pregnancy, breastfeeding, and menopause. If you are a biological mother, your sex life may well have been affected by the well-being that often results from increased estrogen levels during pregnancy, and the fatigue that results from the dramatic decrease in estrogen postpartum.

The biggest challenge is definitely lack of desire due to physical tiredness and the hormonal changes resulting from on-demand breastfeeding. Before I was pregnant, my desire was directly affected by my fertility cycle, and now that I am not ovulating, things are different.

GIVE ME ESTROGEN! I would like to WANT sex again, not just want to make my husband happy.

Hormones will affect you sexually whether they're manufactured in your body or prescribed. If you are post-menopausal, or if you're combating long-term depression, you may find that taking testosterone reinvigorates a waning sexual appetite.

Chronic depression over the last year, and changing medications twice (I had been stabilized before on Prozac, which didn't work any more after two years) completely destroyed any vestige of a sex drive. I'm now taking two grains of testosterone daily to see if I can get it back!

If you use contraceptives containing progesterone (birth control pills, Depo-Provera, Norplant), you may experience a sexually depressing effect.

The first few weeks postpartum were a sexual awakening of sorts because it was the first time in my menstruating life that I wasn't on some sort of birth control or hormone, and wow did I feel great. I would have had sex five times a day if my husband had wanted to. But then sadly came the inevitable, and after the Depo shot I haven't felt like having sex more than once a week.

While we encourage you to investigate the impact of hormones on your sexual well-being, we'd also urge you not to assign an exaggerated power to these biochemical messengers. Physiology is only one of the many factors that affect how sexually desirous—and desirable—you feel. Stress, self-esteem, depression, body image, fatigue, being single, being partnered, and access to time, space, and privacy all impact your libido. Again, context is everything.

My sex drive increased after the birth of my first child. I felt empowered by the birth process and proud at the great job I was doing raising my boy. I was also less tolerant of nonsense in my life. All these things led to greater self-esteem, therefore greater sex drive.

Desire Essentials

I do not have the desire to have sex. I really wish that I could. I really miss that feeling.

I have a newfound zest for sex. I have no idea why, or how it came about. I just hope that it stays!

Like the women quoted above, you may think of desire as a mysterious force outside your control. Weeks or even months can pass by without your thinking much about sex, then one sunny afternoon you catch sight of a cute butt on the bus and it all comes rushing back to you. Desire may feel like a random gift from fickle gods, but it's actually more like the lottery ticket in this old joke: A man gets on his knees day after day, always with the same prayer, "God please let me win the lottery, just let me win the lottery." Finally one day, after months of this routine, he's answered by a voice from the clouds saying, "Abe, meet me halfway—buy a lottery ticket!"

You're not going to feel desire unless you allow yourself to feel it. We like to conceive of desire as an instinctual passion that wells up and sweeps away all obstacles in its path. Sometimes—particularly in the first flush of a new romance—desire does feel like a force of nature. However, most of the time we aren't able to access our oh-so-primal urges unless our hearts and minds are in it, and the fact is, our hearts and minds are designed to generate inhibitors. Motherhood is a mother lode of situational inhibitors in and of itself. But don't despair—becoming conscious of common obstacles to desire is the first step toward making an end run around them. If you can satisfy all of the following prerequisites, you'll be well on your way to hitting your own erotic jackpot.

You have to feel that sex is worthwhile
To want to be sexual, you have to believe that sex is a worthwhile activity. We get conflicting messages in our society: on the one hand, sex is treated like an important status symbol ("My sex life is bigger and better than the Jones's"), and on the other it's treated like a waste of time ("Those shiftless Joneses are never going to get ahead if they spend all their time in the sack"). Either way, sex is rarely presented as a valuable means of self-expression. When you're a busy mother, it's easy to view sex as a luxury that demands time, energy, and resources you don't have to spare. But feeling temporarily unable to motivate around sex is different from feeling that sex is fundamentally frivolous. Eroticism is a necessity. Whenever you feel the surge of sexual desire, you're experiencing connection: a connection of body and mind; a connection to your own emotions, drives, and fantasies; a connection to other people; and, a connection to something outside yourself. If you acknowledge sex as intrinsically meaningful, you'll always be receptive to the tug of desire.

You have to feel that you deserve sexual pleasure
Many of us struggle with internalized scripts about how we're not entitled to sexual pleasure. It's difficult to muster up much desire if you feel fundamentally unworthy. Some women feel ashamed of their sexual inexperience, while others feel equally ashamed of their experience.

> I need to hold on to the idea that I deserve to be held, loved, appreciated, kissed, hugged, and all that. Here in the south, the pervasive attitude toward single moms is, "you made your bed, now lie in it." On bad days, it is easy to adopt that attitude myself. I remind myself that I am twenty-three and beautiful, and just as worthy of love as before my "moral downfall."

Mothers face particular pressure to sublimate all personal urges and focus on developing a purely selfless persona.

> There is a certain amount of self-involved vanity which goes hand-in-hand with feeling sexual. Now that I've got children, I've become so fucking Mother Theresa that getting off is damn near impossible.

Yes, sex is deeply selfish. Sexual self-expression is selfish just as creative self-expression is selfish. Do you really want to go through life without either? Feeling that you're not entitled to be sexual is like feeling you're not entitled to be fully human. Why not choose to explore and express every aspect of yourself?

You have to feel desirable
Concerns about physical appearance often derail women's desire. In fact, it's common for women to tell themselves that they will feel perfectly entitled to sexual pleasure as soon as they make themselves presentable—the "If I just lose five pounds, I'll feel more like having sex" syndrome.

> Body image makes all the difference between whether I want sex or not. I know it sounds weak, but if I don't feel sexy then I don't wanna have sex.

Needless to say, attitude is everything. If you're dealing with a deep sense of dissatisfaction with yourself, it will be impossible for you to feel desirable for long, even if you're showered with constant praise. Plenty of beautiful women are too insecure to be relaxed about sex, and plenty of ordinary looking women are secure in their appeal. Feeling desirable is a matter of confidence and perspective. Most of us find it easiest to access desire when we're feeling healthy, strong, and in harmony with our bodies.

> My biggest turn on is nothing external but rather when I've been treating myself right and feel good in my body.

When you're partnered, you often specifically need to feel desired by your partner. It's usually more important that the person who's most intimate with you finds you desirable than that you get hit on at a party (not that that isn't nice too). Of course, sometimes feeling desirable is inextricable from feeling desire. If your erotic appetites and imagination aren't being stimulated by your environment, they may decline.

> I recently moved to a more repressed town, and I don't think of anyone here in a very sexual manner (except my partner). I find that there just seem to be fewer people I find attractive, which somehow reduces my own interest in sex.

You have to have your own space

Many of us think of "sex" as a sub-category of "relationships," as something we do with or for a partner. But you're a sexual being even if you never "have sex" with another person in your life. You're much more likely to access your truest desires if you have private time and space to explore what makes you tick erotically.

> I need enough time to myself to let my sexuality flourish, rather than clear-cutting it to make room for other peoples' needs and demands.

> What would satisfy me? A quiet room ALONE. Two words: SHOWER MASSAGER.

You have to feel that your desires deserve respect

It's difficult to feel motivated sexually if you don't expect to get what you want out of the encounter. Too often, we go through our lives as sexual adults in reactive mode: soliciting, responding to, or accommodating our partners' desires. Mothers—who are expected to thrive in the role of solicitous, responsive, accommodating caretaker—have to make an extra effort to assert their own erotic needs. You may have a hard time naming your own desires because they seem so unmaternal.

> When I do feel like changing our routine sex, the role of sex initiator still feels incompatible with the role of mummy. I think my biggest challenge is to try and make the two roles exist together. Can mums be sexy?

Or you may find that becoming a mother has both boosted your self-esteem and reduced your tolerance for pussy-footing around!

> I have a much easier time with my sexuality now that I am a mom. I feel stronger and am more able to see that my needs are met. I am also more honest about when I do or do not want to have sex.

Then again, you may have no trouble accepting your theoretical right to be sexual, but have a harder time accepting your right to do the specific things you want to do. If you feel that your sexual desires are somehow ridiculous, "kinky," or otherwise "abnormal," you're likely to do what you can to suppress them, which means your interest in any kind of sex will fade. Throughout this book, we emphasize the utter futility of distinguishing between "normal" and "abnormal" sexual desires. After all, the only norm you can count on is that any sexual activity you could come up with has been considered normal at some time and place in history, and has been considered equally abnormal at some other time and place in history. However, the fact remains that if you're interested in exploring certain fantasies or activities and your partner is not, you'll need to come up with an explicit mutual compromise to avoid short-circuiting your desire. See the Talking to Your Partner about Sex chapter and the Fanning the Flames of Desire chapter for more on this subject.

You have to accept contradictions

By now you may be thinking: "wait a minute. I've actually been in relationships where my self-esteem was low, I had no personal space, and my desires weren't particularly catered to ... but I couldn't get enough of the insensitive jerk who was my lover." Well, we did warn you that desire is complicated. If you honestly appraise your sexual history, you'll doubtless discover what psychotherapist Jack Morin has termed "the paradoxical perspective … that anything that inhibits arousal—including anxiety or guilt—can, under different circumstances, amplify it."[5] For sex to be desirable, there has to be something in it for you, so even if you've been in the classic "woman who loves too much" relationship, it's likely that you were accessing important aspects of your sexual self. If you can tease out the individual components of every highly-arousing situation, and identify what Morin calls your "Core Erotic Theme," you have information you can use to channel your desires into new and healthier avenues of pleasure (his book *The Erotic Mind* is a particularly useful tool). Perhaps you repeatedly find yourself in situations of unrequited love because you get an erotic charge from sensations of longing and uncertainty, in which case you can work toward incorporating elements of anticipation and unpredictability into a relationship with a more reliable partner.

While we don't argue that sexual desires have the ability to make total losers seem ineffably desirable and total winners seem unaccountably unappealing, we are by no means implying that you should strive to repress your desires. For one thing, you simply can't do it, and for another you have so much more to gain if you take the risk of erotic self-exploration. Nor are we implying that some desires are automatically "inappropriate" for mothers, as the survey respondent below seems to feel.

I'm not sure I like the fact that I don't really dig nice, sensual love-making and instead want the dirty, "who's your daddy" sex. Maybe having a daughter and hoping to give her a healthy attitude about sex has made me wonder about my own. I'm sure this has a lot more to do with my pre-baby history.

If you bring consciousness to bear on what it is that fuels your flame, you'll increase both your sexual pleasure and your self-knowledge. These are powerful examples to set for your children.

I'm able to separate my mother role from my lover role and let go of the hang ups that one might think go along with parenting. By that, I mean, if my partner and I want to role play a scene in which one of us is young and one is old, I can separate fantasy from reality, whereas if I thought there was any chance someone would hurt my kids, I would be one hell of a bitch to deal with.

Hot Tips: Inspire Your Desire

As any aspiring actor could tell you, "You've got to know your motivation." When you're yearning for sex, what is it that you're yearning for? If you understand what you get out of sex, you'll be in a better position to figure out what your desire motivators are.

- Pursue pleasure. Sex feels good. Good sex grounds us in our bodies, places us in the moment, and suffuses us with a sense of well-being. And the physical release of orgasm is nothing to sneeze at either.
- Revel in the sensuality. Sex involves physical touch. When we're aroused, our entire body is exquisitely sensitive to tactile stimulation. For many people, a sexual encounter is one of their only opportunities to enjoy flesh-to-flesh contact with another adult.
- Gain validation. Sex is an ego boost—who doesn't enjoy reveling in her body's potential for pleasure during masturbation or feeling desired, appreciated, and catered to during partner sex? The flip side is that it's a great way to express desire and appreciation for someone else.
- Deepen the relationship. Sex creates an emotional connection. When you're engaged in a mutually pleasurable sexual encounter, you can enjoy a deeply satisfying sense of harmony.
- Seek transcendence. Sex takes you out of yourself. You can simultaneously experience total self-awareness and a total lack of self-consciousness.
- Facilitate self-expression. Sex integrates your body, mind, emotions, fantasies, past, present, and future in a way that is utterly unique.

Let It Flow

Probably the most common source of anxiety about desire is an anxiety of quantity—you've surely felt at some times in your life that you had "too much" sexual desire, and at others that you had "too little." Well, Goldilocks, pull up a chair and eat as much porridge as you please. The truth is, however much desire you're feeling at any given moment is probably "just right." While everything you'll read in this book is an encouragement to be sexual, you must express that sexuality on your own terms. Keep in mind that sexual lust is just one aspect of an overall lust for life. Hormones ebb and flow, life situations change, but you are by definition a sexual being. You get to decide what that means to you.

Sex is a part of who I am and not something I simply do. I remain myself and a sensual being just as much after kids as before.

5

Talking to Your Partner
about Sex

"Use your words." We repeat this simple phrase constantly to young children as they learn to speak. We offer it up like a gift, knowing that words will help them move beyond frustrated tears to a place of comfort and understanding. And yet, we who have mastered the art of language, too often don't heed our own advice. We may not stomp our feet and throw tantrums, but we do the adult equivalent: we clam up when we're angry, hurt, frustrated or just plain tired.

Good relationships—whether with lovers, friends, relatives, or children—are not possible without good communication. There's no denying that it's hard work; communication demands courage, empathy, and practice. When it comes to sexual communication, the challenges are even greater, largely because sex is a subject that has been off limits for most of our lives. But your success sustaining an intimate relationship depends on your ability both to listen and to express yourself effectively.

Not Tonight Dear, There's a Baby in the Bed

Motherhood changes your life so profoundly that, particularly if you're in a long-term, coparenting relationship, your sex life can't possibly survive without clear, candid communication. Even if you and your partner see eye to eye on your parenting decisions, you'll need to touch base with each other on an ongoing basis about the impact these decisions have on your sex life. For example, you may both be philosophically committed to the importance of family bed, but if one of you starts to resent the effect the little one's proximity is having on your sex life, you'll need to revisit the subject. How successfully you navigate potentially rocky terrain depends to some degree on how effectively you communicated before the baby was born, but you shouldn't feel limited by your past successes or failures. Many couples find that parenthood actually equips them with new tools that enable and enhance better sexual communication.

Growing up

Let's face it: parenthood forces us to grow up. With a child's life hanging in the balance, we trade in our own childishness for responsibility and accountability. As this survey respondent so eloquently notes, many of the qualities required for good parenting also come in handy in the bedroom.

> To resolve sexual issues takes honesty, strength, flexibility, understanding, listening skills, and other attributes that are definitely important when being a parent.

> The day-to-day realities of parenting require a high degree of communication, which makes for good practice when negotiating sexual concerns.

> Parenthood forced us to finally become really excellent communicators since we've had to settle so many conflicts over little and enormous things. A lot of sex issues between us have been resolved as a result of improved self-expression.

Having to curb hot-headed emotions because there are children present has also led many parents to adopt a more disciplined approach to communication.

> When we disagree now, the strongest effort is made to talk things out calmly and rationally with complete respect for the other's side of the argument. Emotions are controlled, shouting is nonexistent, and complications are smoothed over quickly (most of the time).

Finding your voice

To be heard amidst the cacophony of demands emanating from children and partners, many mothers learn how to speak up for themselves. This new-found assertiveness finds its way into the bedroom as well.

> I'm bolder and more forward with what I want. As a mother I learned that so much of the attention was focused on the baby that if I didn't speak for myself, no one would.

> I have stopped being a wimp because my happiness reflects directly onto my son's life. So if things are uncomfortable in our relationship (sexual or non-sexual issues) I have the motivation to stand up and speak out about it, instead of just shrugging it off. I find being a parent empowering.

We want to underscore the value of this self-advocacy, especially in the face of our cultural tendency to encourage passivity and submissiveness in women. The physical and emotional upheavals of motherhood can catch both you and your partner off guard. If you don't make a point of standing up for your desires, they'll all too easily get lost in the shuffle, while if you prioritize communicating your own needs, you're more likely to achieve a mutually satisfying and respectful relationship.

> I am much more apt to say "do like this" or "let's try this" now than I ever was before. I feel so much more active. Being a mom has made me so courageous about a lot of things and this is just another. My husband has responded well even though getting used to it was shocking for him. He's been so much more supportive over all ever since I learned how to ask for things instead of waiting for him to give them to me.

Time is too precious

Some parents explain that the frantic pace of their lives, coupled with the desire to maintain a peaceful environment for their children, forces them to deal with issues expediently.

> I need constant communication. Even if it's too much at times, even if it just amounts to venting frustrations, it's completely necessary

now. There is no time to waste being angry or having problems and not talking about them.

I think our communication has actually gotten better because we have more motivation for making sure our relationship thrives. We don't want bad vibes passed on to the baby.

Precisely because there is less time available to spend with a partner, some parents find that good communication enhances a long-awaited erotic encounter.

We have spent a lot more time talking about what we enjoy and what we would like to try than we did before the baby. We want to make the periods of time we have for sex the best they can be.

The flip side
Of course we don't expect you to believe that parenthood has magically transformed every mother but you into an eloquent speaker whose every word is perfectly understood, and whose every need is thereby fulfilled. Feeling pressed for time and privacy can inhibit you from dealing with difficult issues at least as often as it inspires you to resolve them.

My husband and I are both a little uneasy about talking directly about sex and our emotional relationship. The baby serves as an easy excuse not to confront issues.

We are silent much more because we fear we will say something that may cause an argument and we both know we don't have time to fight.

Before the baby, you and your partner may have been so connected you were able to finish each other's thoughts, but now your changing lives may leave you somewhat out of synch.

We used to think like one person, even finishing each other's sentences. Now we're on two different planets. The communication issues make it really difficult for me to feel intimate, and for me intimacy is a precursor to sex. He doesn't have this problem, but I know he feels unattractive and like I don't want to have sex with him.

Even if parenthood has taught us to grow up, to advocate for ourselves, and to make better use of our time, we may still be overwhelmed by the sheer number of issues that require discussion. Before we explore just how to communicate more effectively, let's examine the roots of our difficulty talking about sex.

Hot Tips: *Tell Me About It*

When asked to name the most common challenges to their sex lives since becoming parents, our survey respondents most often cited: lack of desire or desire discrepancies, body image, contraception and safer sex, conflicts over division of labor, sexual boredom, and difficulty negotiating sexual encounters. Take these examples:

- My husband doesn't understand my complete lack of desire.
- It is difficult with a new lover because of my poor self-image.
- It's hard for her to understand how tired I am.
- He's tired of me not being in the mood.
- He thinks I am not someone to be dating since I am a mom now.
- It has been difficult trying to explain why things have changed.
- I know he feels unattractive and that I don't want to have sex with him.
- He feels left out justifiably and I feel like I'm carrying the load on my own.
- I am afraid to tell my husband how little I care about sex.
- All he hears is me bitching.

All these frustrated women—and their partners—would benefit from applying a little more effort or a new approach to communication. Sure, some of the issues implicit in these complaints (waning desire, poor body image) can't be resolved with a simple chat—we address these specific problem areas in more detail throughout this book. But every one of these issues is less likely to depress and demoralize you if you can express your feelings and concerns effectively.

Why We Keep Our Mouths Shut

Plenty of well-spoken people are speechless when it comes to sex. It may not appear that way at first blush—witness the talk show host leering over "sisters who sleep with each other's boyfriends," the lawyer eloquently prosecuting a sex offender, or a newspaper columnist making a case for porn's first amendment rights. But listen closely to what's being said and you will hear every emotion from out-and-out hysteria to clinical detachment, but no personal expressions of authentic sexual feeling. We see sexual imagery all around us, but when was the last time you told your partner everything about his or her body that turns you on? As a society we are preoccupied with sex, but as individuals we are cowed by it. This disconnect between what we perceive and what we feel leaves many of so confused we are rendered mute when it comes to the subject of sex. How did we get this way?

Cultural legacy of sex-negativity

It's not easy to shrug off thousands of years worth of sex-negativity. We're all raised on a steady diet of stereotypes about sex: that nice girls don't have it, that boys like sex and girls like romance, or that sex is either a reproductive necessity or a shameful pleasure. As a result we live in a society of fairly ignorant and repressed sexual adults whose fascination with what has been hidden, forbidden, or denounced throughout their lives now drives a sex-obsessed economy. But this economy only reflects our collective checkered past and reveals the extent of our fundamental discomfort with sex. Although sex sells everything from cars to fast food to shampoo, you rarely see ads of any kind for sexual products (condoms, lubricants). Although TV shows and music videos depict kids dressing, acting, and looking mighty sexy, we balk at the idea of condom dispensers in schools. Sex rarely makes the news unless it topples a political figure or is the subject of an editorial on society's moral decay.

Where are the testimonials from individuals who have experienced first hand the life-affirming, joyous qualities of sex? These women and men are out there, but given the jokes, threats, finger-pointing, and condescension that would greet their testimonials, few have the combination of courage and thick skin it takes to stand up for sexual pleasure in our sex-negative culture. It's easier to keep quiet, and by default perpetuate the notion that sex is something best not talked about.

Poor sex education

America's sexual dysfunction manifests itself most disturbingly in our inability to provide adequate sex education to our young people. Most of us received little more than a cursory lesson in reproductive biology during our youth; today's kids get bonus lectures in safe sex that contrast abstinence with dire alternatives (death, disease, despair). Kids are rarely taught about sexual responsibility, assertiveness, or technique, yet they are expected to mature into sexually-fulfilled adults at an arbitrary age determined by their state, parents, or church. The following quote underscores the fallacy of this notion, and the fact that learning to communicate about sex is a life-long process.

> I'm thirty-eight and have been dating a bit. I swear though, I feel like I'm an adolescent—I'm surprised at how much pressure there is to have sex, and how hard it is to speak up for myself and to stay clear about my boundaries.

No role models

Given that most of us were raised believing we shouldn't talk about sex, it's no wonder we find it a daunting task. Don't look to Hollywood for role-modeling of sexual communication—when was the last time you saw TV or movie characters discuss contraception, or pause a sex scene to say "a little to the left, and not so fast!" Chances are your parents weren't exactly ideal role models, even if they had good intentions:

> My mother said she would be open to talking to me and my sister yet she wasn't really. I never went to her because I could sense she was uncomfortable about it. I really hope to be easy for my daughters to talk to, so I make a point of being there for my much younger sisters (nineteen, fifteen and eleven) to talk to about sex and their relationships. I hope that by doing this I can be ready to talk to my own daughters.

This mom recognizes the value of modeling positive sexual communication. By participating in an open and honest dialogue about sex with the young people in her life, she is giving them the tools to do the same with future partners.

Lack of sexual self-awareness

Inadequate sex education affects sexual communication in another very fundamental way. If you are unfamiliar with your sexual anatomy or your own sexual responses, you will understandably have trouble telling a partner what pleases you sexually. Or if you have mistaken beliefs about what's sexually "normal," you may be too confused by or ashamed of your responses to discuss them. For example, we've talked to countless women frustrated by their inability to orgasm during intercourse. Many had no idea that the majority of women orgasm through clitoral stimulation—an area not typically stimulated during intercourse. Since girls are often not taught the correct names for their genitals, or taught to regard them with distaste or disapproval, it's no surprise that they grown up into adults who aren't sure what an orgasm is or how to reach one.

If you could use a little Sex Ed 101, see the Resources section for our recommendations on books and videos designed to help you better understand your sexuality. In addition, we recommend masturbation as the best way to learn about your sexual responses.

Language barriers

Some people are literally unable to talk about sex because they're uncomfortable with sexual terminology. Perhaps you find words like "vagina" and "penis" too clinical, but words like "cunt" and "cock" too crass. Try to figure out what words you're uncomfortable with and why, and explain this to your partner. The two of you can choose to avoid certain words, to make up new ones, or to work on overcoming your aversion. Self-help books like *Talk Sexy to the One You Love* include lists of terms you can try on for size. If you'd like to expand your comfort level with sexual terminology, try repeating certain words out loud by yourself when alone—this will make them more familiar and rob them of some of their awkwardness.

> After my sister and I read *The Vagina Monologues*, we decided it was time to get over our shyness about anatomical terms. Now my sister will call me up and say, "Vagina, vagina, vagina" over the phone until we both start laughing.

Watch an erotic video or read some erotica in order to expose yourself to a range of sexually-explicit language. Read up on the origin of the word as a way of finding something sexy about it—perhaps its etymology will inspire you. For example, "dildo" comes from the Italian "diletto", which means delight. Now you have the option of using the sexy Italian version or merely delighting in the original!

Our histories

Each of us brings our entire past to every relationship. Our unique approach to sexual relationships is shaped by a lifetime of social conditioning, religious upbringing, family values, and past sexual experiences. Sharing information about your past with your partner gives you both a valuable context for the issues that may arise in your sex life. For example, if this mom communicates about her past sexual abuse, she can provide her partner with crucial insights into how it affects her experience of intimacy and parenting.

> Before I was a mom I was in deep denial about my past, but becoming a mother has put me face to face with my demons. Also, being the mother of a little girl has brought up a lot—I aspire to help her be strong and find her own voice so she isn't victimized as I was.

Fear

Perhaps the most frequently cited reason for poor sexual communication is fear. We're afraid of hurting, insulting, threatening, or displeasing a partner. We're afraid of embarrassing ourselves or of being rejected.

> It's very hard for us to communicate about the problems we've been having with sex, as it seems one or both of us get our feelings hurt when we try.

It's absolutely true that discussing sex with a partner can inspire emotional reactions that neither of you enjoy. But it's also true that if you don't take this risk, you'll never get beyond whatever stalemate you're stuck in. Communication is the only catalyst for change, and if you follow some of the basic techniques we present in the next section, any initial awkwardness and hurt feelings can be transformed to a new and greater understanding.

Say It Loud, Say It Proud

When it comes to communication, a little effort and a lot of patience go a long way. Try some of these basic pointers to start an ongoing dialogue about sex.

Make time
One of the biggest complaints voiced by mothers is lack of time. With every hour of your day accounted for, intangible tasks like "communication" fall by the wayside.

> The children require 110% of everything: our time, attention, thoughts, worries. Everything else is shoved way down on the list, including our interaction with each other.

> We definitely have less time to communicate and because of this our different communication styles are more of an issue—and source of tension. This is a far greater change than any specific sexual issue.

If your partner is your coparent, you probably do most of your communicating on the fly. You need to supplement these brief exchanges by setting aside time for quality conversations that cover a wide range of topics. Couples often find that until they air and resolve differences about nonsexual issues, they have little motivation to deal with sex.

> If there are issues that really need to be resolved, I can't put them aside and have sex with the person I am angry with/at odds with. Needless to say, my husband is not happy with this situation, and we are trying to find ways to not let this happen. I have to find ways to talk with him before we're in bed, and he has to see to it that issues are resolved before he puts the moves on me.

The flip side is that good communication about day-to-day topics paves the way for a more fulfilling sex life.

> We never put sex ahead of communication. Even a tiny unresolved issue can put a damper on the sexual fires. We usually talk about our day—issues, concerns, etc.—just after work or before sex. We find

that if we are comfortable with our lives and each other that sex is so much more intimate.

The most important thing about prioritizing sex is to keep talking with your partner about your needs. They may not get fulfilled that minute, but if I make my needs known, they can be fulfilled sooner rather than later!

Make sex talk a priority
Just as you have to plan for sex, you have to plan to talk about sex. Whether you're embarking on a regimen to get more comfortable with sexual subject matter (see the following section) or you have specific issues you need to discuss, you'll benefit from advance planning. Pick a time that's convenient for both of you, rather than cornering your partner into a surprise talk. "Honey, could we set aside some time to talk about our sex life?" will be a more effective way to start the dialogue than, "We need to talk about sex now because I'm miserable."

If you are disappointed or frustrated by your sexual encounters, avoid venting your feelings in the heat of the moment. It's hard to be rational, empathetic, and focused when you're reeling from a failed sexual encounter or a sexual rejection. Wait a day or two and then raise the subject. While time can bring perspective, it can also bring complacency and denial—make sure you address any issues that still bother you, rather than trying to convince yourself that they aren't really that important.

When the time comes for your sex talk, don't stray from your topic. Avoid switching midstream into an argument about who should pick the kids up from school. Of course there will be overlap, because issues in your everyday life affect your sex drive; just keep the conversation relevant to your sex life. If you do find that your bottom line is, "I have no energy for sex because I'm chasing the baby all day," make that clear and ask for help.

Hot Tips: Bringing Up Sex

If only sex were as easy to talk about as the weather, many of our sexual communication issues would disappear. Can you imagine this idle remark over coffee: "I'm thinking today is a mutual masturbation day." Perhaps if we had more practice talking about sex, we wouldn't be so reticent to bring up the subject. By regularly engaging in conversations about sex, you become more comfortable with the subject matter and you get to learn about your partner's views. Your sex life needn't be the focus of each discussion, in fact it's probably easier to start with less threatening subjects. Here are a few suggestions for steering the subject toward sex:

- Comment on sex-related issues in the news.
- Bring up a subject from a daytime talk show (they almost all involve sex).
- Share amusing sex comments from your toddler.
- Share sex histories.
- Relate messages you received about sex as a child.
- Hum the tune from a sexy song, ask your partner to name some sexy music.
- Describe your favorite sex scene from a movie.
- Read a sexual enhancement book and share your findings.
- Look at some erotic art together.
- Share a favorite fantasy.
- Read erotica together.

Know the issues/be prepared

It's so much easier to get what you want when you know what you want. Shopping is a cinch when you've got a list, a visit to the doctor's office is more productive when you can describe your symptoms, and a raise can be negotiated more effectively when you know what you're worth. So before you approach any conversation about sex with your partner, think about what it is you want or need, imagine how your partner might feel, and be prepared to suggest some action.

If you're feeling vague dissatisfaction with your sex life, you need to pin down the specific source of your unhappiness. If it's physical—perhaps you don't orgasm when or how you'd like—stop thinking of this as all your partner's fault. Take the time to figure out what gives you pleasure during masturbation and partner sex, and you'll be able to tell your partner what stimulation works best for you. If you're experiencing emotional dissatisfaction, start by identifying what's troubling you. If you're feeling ignored, taken for granted, or angry, come up with specific examples to illustrate how your partner is (and isn't) contributing to your dissatisfaction, and think about what steps you could both take to address it. It may help one or both of you to seek therapy to get to the root of your problems.

It's important to be clear on your own desires, but equally important to try to see the situation from your partner's perspective. If you can explore both sides of an issue before you discuss it, you may be able to get a jump-start on the empathy that's a prerequisite to constructive communication. Sometimes it's very easy to resolve what has seemed like a major source of tension; for example, this woman's partner simply needed reassurance that her fatigue wasn't a personal rejection.

> It was initially hard for my husband to understand how tired I was and that sex was literally the last thing on my mind. I had to convince him that I was not rejecting him and that it was a passing phase.

Hot Tips: Talking with a Doctor

Perhaps even more difficult than talking to your partner about sex is approaching your health care practitioner about a sexual concern. With many HMOs allotting fifteen minutes for routine visits, you've got a pretty small window in which to self-advocate. Make the most of your visit by following these tips:

- Make a list. Jot your questions down in advance instead of expecting to remember them at the appointment.
- Do your homework. Research your questions in advance from other sources (the Web, books, peers) to inform your discussion, and to offer your provider an opportunity to debunk any misinformation.
- Be specific. "I itch down there" will get you started, but "My entire vulva itches and is inflamed after sex with a latex condom, but there's no discharge or smell" will give your practitioner more to go on.
- Practice at home. If you're afraid you might chicken out, practice on a partner or a friend beforehand. As a last resort, write down your questions (along with your name and phone number) and hand this over during the appointment.
- Call in the cavalry. Bring along a partner or a friend, who can either provide support or pinch hit for you if you get tongue-tied.

> • Be accessible. If your practitioner can't answer your questions
>   during the appointment, make it easy for her or him to get back
>   to you. Leave phone and email contact information, and offer to
>   call back at an agreed upon time.
> • Request more time. If you've got a lot of questions, request a
>   longer time slot when making your appointment.

Be direct and clear

Forget the fantasy that the perfect lover will intuit all your sexual needs and supply you with orgasms till dawn. A good lover knows how to observe a partner's reactions and ask what feels good, but he or she can't read minds. Give your partner a hand by clearly explaining your needs. Instead of saying, "I want more foreplay," be as specific as you can: "If you could spend more time kissing me, massaging my thighs, and whispering in my ear, I'd have a lot more energy to take you on with."

Similarly, when you're in the throes of passion, don't rely solely on nonverbal communication to express your pleasure or displeasure. Not everyone is adept at reading body language (especially if they're concentrating on what they're doing!), so offer a few verbal cues such as, "Oh that feels great," or "Don't move an inch," or "It feels best when you stop and start." This will give your partner some appreciated encouragement and net you a more satisfying encounter.

Make sure to define your terms. To you, "I just don't feel much desire these days" might mean that you don't crave lengthy sex marathons, but to your partner, it might sound like, "I just don't find you attractive anymore."

> Sometimes I need to make it clear to my partner that it is not that I
> don't want sex with him, it's just that it is hard to relax knowing that
> our daughter might crawl into the room at any time.

Give as much information as you can about your feelings, and try to provide context. Rather than rejecting a partner's request for sex outright, take the time to explain what's affecting your loss of libido, what sorts of things can boost your sex drive, and how you would like to proceed. You may reveal something from your sexual history or current experience that helps your partner understand your position. Ultimately, your goal is to clarify your issues in order to negotiate a solution.

Directness serves you equally well whether you're entering into a new sexual relationship or fine-tuning an existing one.

> Now that I'm a mom and single again, I don't want any relationship other than physical, and I communicate that very openly.

> We found we had to be much clearer because spontaneity is so much harder. For example on a Saturday night I might say to my husband, "Honey, tomorrow morning when Ruby goes down for her morning nap we have GOT to have sex!" This kind of directness was not as necessary before we were parents.

Minimize the negative

No one responds well to the verbal equivalent of a finger-wagging, so avoid attacking or blaming your partner. The best way to do this is to use "I" statements to convey your feelings. For example, the statement "I feel pressured to have sex" is a natural opening to a discussion of the many sources of pressures in your life (yourself, your partner, or your life), but the statement "You're always pressuring me to have sex" lays all the blame at your partner's feet. Similarly, trade in the criticism for some helpful suggestions, and make sure to use positive reinforcement when your partner makes an effort. You might think she gives a lousy massage, but instead of blurting out "That feels terrible," pick up a massage book and a bottle of oil, then try this approach: "I love it when you touch me, so I thought we could try learning more about massage. Would you be up for trying out a few techniques?" Finally, eliminate those negative absolutes from your vocabulary. Rather than saying, "I never come when you suck my clit," or "You always rush through oral sex," how about, "It feels best when you lick my clit, especially when you circle it slowly with your tongue."

Be a good listener

It's not enough to express yourself well—a successful conversation depends on your being a good listener. Listening may sound easier than it is; in fact there are several skills you'll want to hone in this department. First and foremost, good listening requires that you stay present during the conversation (no daydreaming). This means you have to recognize when you're too tired to be fully present and postpone your talk as necessary. You may also find it helpful to practice what's known as "active listening." When you partner is through speaking, repeat back what you heard and ask if you got it right. This ensures that you've registered and understood what she or he is trying to convey. Perhaps the most difficult aspect of listening is actually letting yourself hear the truth in what your partner has to say. Too often, our knee-jerk response is to defend a position or prove a partner wrong, and we don't stop to examine the legitimacy of his or her claims. Most people can accurately pinpoint how their partner's attitudes and behaviors could be improved, but have a hard time acknowledging areas for self-improvement. Learn from your partner, and don't be afraid to admit when he or she is right; this is an excellent catalyst for change.

Allow for differences
You didn't choose your mate (we hope) because he or she was a carbon copy of you, so don't try to turn him or her into one. Expect disagreement and respect your differences. While you can't force each other to change, the process of communication and compromise can lead to growth and change for both parties.

> Communication issues were really rough the first three years after birth. He just wasn't as tuned into the baby as I was, and I of course thought he did everything wrong. I had to ease up and let him find his way as a parent. We really had to sit down and talk about what we wanted family-wise and sexually. I had to make him talk and search his soul for answers when really he just wished I could decide everything and he could just follow.

Even as your communication skills evolve over the course of a long-term relationship, you'll always have to be willing to embrace the best and accommodate the worst elements of your individual styles.

> My partner always gets me to explain my frustrations and that helps resolve most issues for us. I yell at him sometimes, and he hates that, but we always "finish" a fight. We never leave it hanging there in the air. Because we have such an important connection now, and a very good reason to work things out, we really want to understand each other and "get along."

Hot Tips: Sexy Body Language

Busy schedules and needy kids may preclude long leisurely lovemaking sessions, but you can regularly express affection without ever speaking a word. Affectionate touch can go along way toward reassuring your partner. Here are a few suggestions for incorporating sexy nonverbal gestures into your daily routine.

- Make eye contact and hold it.
- Make long leisurely kissing a routine part of your hellos and goodbyes.
- Touch gently during conversation—brush the arm, stroke the neck, rub the thigh.
- Sit close together on the couch, or put your head in his or her lap.
- Fall asleep in the spoon position.
- Hold hands.

Negotiate

Communication won't be worth the energy you expend if you're bent on defending your position at all costs. You might as well be shouting at the moon. It's fine to disagree with your partner, but you must be willing to work out a solution that will satisfy you both. This is where the fine art of compromise comes into to play. Elsewhere in this book, we suggest ways to negotiate common sexual issues (see the Fanning the Flames of Desire Chapter), but for now we offer a fine example of the rewards of a little mutual back-scratching.

> We've agreed that it is too easy to "forget" to have sex, and that we are both equally responsible for making sure we both get what we need. If I want to get laid, I make sure the kids go to bed and then I dress in a favorite bit of lingerie and the rest is history. If hubby wants a bit, he either negotiates a blow job (I trade for an extra hour of sleep in the morning, which is what I really need) or he shaves and kisses the back of my neck. We've been pretty good about not saying no when the other person has made the effort to ask in these ways.

Get help

Don't feel you have to wait until you're at your wits' end to seek professional help. If you and your partner struggle with disagreements, standoffs, and a chronic inability to meet each other half way, you could benefit from counseling. While many couples are resistant to go into couples' therapy because they see it as an admission that the relationship has failed (or is about to go down in flames), therapy can actually enable you to take your relationship to a deeper level of honesty and acceptance. A good therapist is an unbiased third party who can help you distinguish between projection, expectation, and reality and make you aware of the individual blind spots that are impeding your communication. We've listed some relevant professional organizations, along with some recommended self-help books in the Resources section.

Sex Is Communication

> Sex is such an important part of our relationship, it's another road of communication for us.

We would be remiss if we left this chapter without pointing out the simple truth that sex is communication. Sexual intimacy allows us to express desire, love, vulnerability, and a host of other complex emotions. The language of sex cannot be adequately described with words, or replaced with other types of conversation. We have used this chapter to promote communication as a requirement for good sex, but good sex becomes its own type of profound communication. Who needs more incentive than that?

6

Having It All:
Sex, Sanity and Sleep

There's nothing like having a child in your life to make you realize what an abundance of everything you had when you were without one. Sleep, time, energy, even friends seemed more plentiful in those long ago lazy days. Being in love, enjoying sex alone or with partners—it all flowed so naturally and effortlessly because you only had to think and act for yourself. But kids enter your life with all the impact of a hurricane, blowing out the routines and self-indulgences, leaving you to weather a new regime of scarcity and self-sacrifice.

> There will never again be enough time, energy, privacy, etc. once you become a mom. You must claw and scratch for every last moment.

Bleak as it sounds, calmer winds will prevail, particularly if you hone a few survival skills. Navigating the sea of scarcity depends entirely on your ability to take care of yourself. Without this, you can't function effectively as a parent or a loving partner. If you have a hard time reconciling your maternal identity with the perceived "selfishness" of prioritizing your own pleasure, keep in mind that being a wiped out, bedraggled, resentful mom won't benefit your loved ones. Do your family and yourself a favor, and look out for number one.

To that end, this chapter is geared toward helping you find ways to rebalance your time, spontaneity, privacy, and energy. Typically, when these fall by the wayside, so do your chances of a satisfying sex life. And while we recognize that sex may be the last thing on your mind (especially if you're a new mom), continuing to view yourself as a sexual being is an important part of your emotional and physical health. The last thing we want is for sex to become one more pressure-filled goal, but we can help you create space in your hectic life so that basking in a little sensual pleasure is both desirable and easily within reach.

> The quantity of sex has suffered, but the quality is better. It's more special when we do find the time. We're more adventurous and creative in our lovemaking. It's lowered my inhibitions and made me more daring.

> "Lack of spontaneity" is not always bad; I get lots of pleasure in my (very few) spare moments looking forward to Saturday night.

This chapter has a particular focus on negotiating the life changes that result when your children are young, but much of the advice will be useful even as your children grow older. For tips specific to single moms, see the Sex and the Single Mom chapter.

Time: It's No Longer on Your Side

Your experience of time changes in three ways once you have a child: you no longer have enough of it, you start to experience it differently, and you feel like it doesn't really belong to you anymore. Well, sure, you still have the same number of hours in a day, but the demands on your time increase drastically. When you tally up the number of hours spent changing diapers, watching Disney movies, picking up toys, driving kids around, or attending school events, cloning starts to sound like an attractive option. When you're constantly squeezed for time, pastimes like hobbies, exercise and sex come to seem "indulgent" and often get sacrificed unless you make a conscious effort to include them in your routine.

Your experience of time changes perceptibly, particularly when you have young children. You will find that your day can no longer be divided into neat little compartments—work at 9 AM, lunch at noon, cocktails at 6 PM, nookie at 10 PM—because babies couldn't care less about clocks or schedules.

As a result, the relationship between the quality and quantity of time you spend doing any one thing changes dramatically. A morning stroll through the park may appear restful to others, but you'd trade it in a heartbeat for just five minutes alone with the newspaper. There is a silver lining: you learn to stop and smell the roses, your patience threshold goes way up, and you really, really relish what once were simple pleasures. The attitude adjustment you're forced to make translates well into the sexual realm. For example, you learn to take advantage of the sensual moments you find throughout the day; patience will make you a more skillful lover; and something as simple as a passionate kiss can be as erotically thrilling as any midnight rendezvous.

Hot Tips: Gifts Every Mom Can Use

Do your friends, coworkers, or relatives ever say, "Just let me know how I can help out"? Well, photocopy this page and invite them to make good on their offers.

- One night of free baby-sitting. Either you can offer to baby-sit your friend's kid(s) so they can go play with other friends, or you can spring for a baby-sitter so your parent friend can come out and play with you. This gift CANNOT be given too many times! Many of the following suggestions require that baby-sitting be arranged, so go for broke and combine ideas.
- An overnight with your friend's child. Along the same lines as baby-sitting, offering to have the child over for a sleepover gives your friend a much needed morning off.
- A meal at your favorite restaurant. It doesn't have to be fancy to be appreciated. As most parents will tell you, the sheer luxury of eating out without the kids makes even a trip to the local diner highly enjoyable.
- Movie passes or tickets to the theater, opera, dance, etc—whatever you both enjoy.
- Afternoon tea is an elegant ritual that relaxes and rejuvenates. You can host tea yourself and invite others over—all it takes is a variety of teas and a few baked goods, or go splurge at high tea in a hotel or restaurant.
- One video night. You pick up the tape and come over and watch it with your friend after her or his kid has gone to sleep. This one is great because it doesn't require any baby-sitting, but you get to hang out together.
- Drinks at your favorite bar or café. This doesn't cost much but it gets right down to the business of socializing.

It makes sense that time no longer feels like your own considering that the bulk of what you're doing is being done for another person. Many people who cope well with demands on their time in their professional lives find it much more difficult to get their marching orders from children. Not only do the demands come without warning or structure, there's no overtime pay, and no one's going to promote you for doing a great job. Putting another person first—usually without any acknowledgment or reward—is a great sacrifice, and it will suck the life out of you if you don't build in some time to call your own. You don't necessarily need to spend this time alone, but you must spend it the way you want to, and spend it on yourself. Don't free up an hour just so you can go grocery shopping. Use it for sleep, cuddling, masturbation or sex, but use it for something that will relax and rejuvenate you.

Freeing up time

It's entirely possible to squeeze extra minutes, even hours out of your day simply by reviewing your routine with an eye to more efficiency. In some cases, a monetary investment will buy you time (in the form of labor-saving devices or hired help), so if you're short on funds, please consult the sidebar for money-saving tips. Even if you employ only one or two of the following suggestions, you'll be surprised at the difference they can make in your quality of life. If you're a brand-new parent, you may be so overwhelmed by your total loss of control over the day that it's difficult to contemplate efficiency tips. After all, there are days when simply taking a shower is a major achievement. If you can incorporate some of these suggestions before your baby arrives, they'll stand you in good stead. But it's never too late to put any of them into effect.

Get a computer and go on-line

If you live in an urban area and can afford a personal computer (many computer companies offer credit), you're just a "point and click" away from convenient shopping, bill paying, and banking. No more running around town doing errands; it can all be done from the convenience of your home, with the items delivered to your doorstep.

> On-line grocery delivery has changed my life. I can do the shopping at night and my order is delivered to my kitchen the next day. I don't miss lugging all that apple juice and laundry detergent up my stairs!

Hot Tips: Money Saving Ideas

Free up some extra cash and you can hire that babysitter to give yourself and your partner a night out. You can't afford not to!

- Find lower interest rates on credit cards and loans (visit www. lowermybills. com).
- Get a roommate to share expenses or share a house with another parent.
- Buy secondhand clothes, appliances, furniture.
- Bring bag lunches to work.
- Sell your car and take public transportation.
- Give up luxury expenses that you don't really use: cell phones, cable TV, gym memberships.
- Comparison shop on-line for lowest prices, special offers, reduced rates, free shipping, etc.

Hire help
Bring someone in for housecleaning, or pay a neighbor kid to do errands, chores, and gardening. If you're a stay-at-home mom, hire someone to baby-sit one day a week so you can have a day off.

Order take-out
You can always count on pizza and Chinese take-out, or have your partner pick something up on the way home. Let your friends know that sending over casseroles, groceries, or dessert is one of the best gifts they could give a new parent. And thanks to the expanding world of on-line commerce, home-delivery cuisine options may soon know no bounds.

> I was so tired one day I said to hell with dinner. I went on-line and found a vendor who delivered a pint of ice-cream, gourmet sand-wiches, and a CD that I'd been meaning to buy.

Shop and cook in bulk
Instead of going to the supermarket every day, plan your menus in advance and shop once during the week. Similarly, when you cook a meal, make a double batch and freeze some for the future.

Invest in labor-saving appliances

If your apartment or home has the hookups, do whatever it takes to get a dishwasher and washing machine. You don't have to spend much more on reconditioned appliances than you'd spend in a year at the Laundromat. Kids generate a mind boggling amount of dirty clothes and cups—you don't need to spend your time dragging it all to the Tidy Wash or washing baby bottles to the tune of "One Hundred Bottles of Beer on the Wall." And by all means, if you're determined to use cloth diapers, get a diaper service—you'll save a huge amount of time.

Throw out the white gloves

It's time to lower your standards—get used to a little clutter and let the dust-bunnies breed. Probably the number-one tip from our survey respondents is to get comfortable with a little dirt.

> An immaculate house will not matter in the end. It's the time invested in your relationships—with family, with your kids, with your friends, and above all your partner—that matters.

Managing time

These suggestions are specifically geared toward creating time for you and your partner to be together, but some also allow you to create more time alone:

Hot Tips: Time Saving Ideas

Free up a little time so you can spend it with a partner, or indulge yourself in some sensual pleasure:

- Shop on-line.
- Hire help.
- Order takeout.
- Cook extra and freeze it.
- Get labor-saving appliances.
- Clean less often.

Overlap shifts

If you work different shifts so you're rarely home at the same time, try overlapping by an extra half hour, just so you can check in with each other about your day.

Extend day care

Consider leaving your child in school or day care for an extra half hour, while both of you plan to arrive home at the usual time.

Job flexibility

If one or both of your jobs permit, schedule some regular time during the working week to be together, even if it's only during lunch.

> NOONERS! They are the absolutely best thing that has happened to my sex life since my children were born.

> Sometimes while the baby is engrossed in her favorite TV show, which thankfully comes on at my husband's lunch hour, we sneak into the bedroom for a quickie.

Cancel appointments

If one or both of you is heavily scheduled, agree to cancel one appointment each week and spend the time together.

Family nap

Institute a "family nap" during which everyone—including you—goes to their rooms for quiet time. You can explain to the children that you need your privacy or "grown up" time and don't want to be disturbed.

Enforce bedtime

No matter how desperately they plead for one more drink of water, how much they beg for one last TV show, or how charmingly they offer to help you get ready for bed—do not give in to your kids' stall tactics. Enforce regular bedtimes, so you can count on adults-only time. Kids actually thrive on routine, so if you can train them to respect morning privacy too, you're that much better off.

Because of "grown up" time, we are really uptight about bedtime schedules now with the second child. With the oldest we were really lax about schedules and paid dearly by never ever being alone.

My husband fixed the old lock on the bedroom door and on Saturday mornings, we insist to the kids that they respect our time alone while we "have a cup of tea," and they simply have to wait and we'll see to all their needs when we get up. This is of course with older children (seven and five) who have something to do and can understand the request.

Use the media
Take advantage of cartoons, videos or computer games to sneak in a little private time.

Sunday morning cartoons—there can be no other justification for the existence thereof. I say kids should be forced to watch as of age one.

Look for opportunities within your routine
You never know what interesting erotic rituals will be born out of necessity:

My husband and I like to watch certain shows in the evening. If we like the shows that are on at 8:00 and 9:00, but not the one at 8:30, we have sex at 8:30. It works out great.

My husband came up with something we refer to as "the booty call" and it is great. We go to sleep (because we really need it) and he wakes up in the middle of the night and starts to fondle me and whisper to me, which leads to wonderful dreamlike sex.

We took the television out of our bedroom and started just turning the lights off right when we went to bed, so that rather than watch TV or read, we'd be motivated to talk or be intimate.

Vacation at home
You don't need a special occasion to send the kids off to a beloved relative's

house. It creates a fun getaway for your kids and leaves you home alone together with a long stretch of free time.

> Our kids went out of town to stay with relatives (just for fun) and we spent the whole weekend together, just the two of us, enjoying our time and ourselves. It rocked because we almost never got out of bed!

Multi-task

You'd be surprised what you can accomplish, with a little imagination.

> Make the most of your time and energy. We do this by showering together regularly. We can have sex, get cleaned, and lock the doors all at the same time. Take long drives with sleeping children in the car and pull over—hand jobs can be great and discreet. We have yet to have a child wake up on us, and even if they did they couldn't see anything anyway.

Use baby-sitters

Find, use, and appreciate good babysitters—they quite simply are the key to your sanity.

> I know people who have never left their children alone overnight. EVER. And you know what? Their relationships suck! You have to get away. Even for just one night. The best sex my husband and I have had the whole time we've been together is during romantic week-end getaways.

It's never too soon to overcome your reservations about leaving your precious bundle with someone else. If you learn to leave your infant with trusted adults, he or she will grow into a more social, engaging child, and you'll be able to retain some independence. Here are a few options for baby-sitters:

Relatives

If you like your relatives and are lucky enough to have some living nearby, they are an ideal source of (usually) free baby-sitting. Many grandparents, aunts, and uncles can be tapped for an evening, afternoon, or an overnight, and will hopefully thrill at the opportunity to develop a special bond with your child. Older siblings, nieces, and nephews might jump at the chance to be a "grown-up baby-sitter," especially if you throw in some money.

> God bless my mom and dad for those occasional days that they pick our daughter up on their way home from work and take her to their house for dinner.

Friends

Responsible friends and roommates are another source of cheap childcare. Now is the time to take up any offer you ever received from a friend or a coworker to baby-sit. They want to help you out, so let them.

> Schedule in friends who can watch the kids at their house from the time they are little.

Friends without kids might need a little "cultivating" to overcome their anxieties about baby-sitting. Invite them along on a few outings with you and your child so they can observe your routine. Or simply have them over to baby-sit while you relax somewhere else in the house. Make every effort to talk openly about what their concerns are and give heaps of positive reinforcement. And don't be shy about soliciting child care; you can get creative in your approach:

> I told my friends that I didn't want them to buy me presents at birthdays and holidays, but that I'd love coupons good for free baby-sitting or evenings out sans kid.

Other parents

Trade off babysitting with another parent—this costs nothing and gives your child a playmate. But be vigilant about reciprocating! Join a play group or a mothers group to meet other parents, or network with the parents at your child's day care or school.

> Arrange with someone else to swap child care—alternate Saturday nights, or you get Fridays and the other parent(s) get Saturdays. Once a week is way better than hardly ever.

Baby-sitters for hire

Even if you have an active network of family and friends who baby-sit, it's great to have the backup of a paid sitter. Get referrals from other parents, look for ads in parenting magazines, try finding or posting fliers at day care centers, churches, community centers, high schools, and kids' clothing stores. Look for agencies or listings on-line and in the yellow pages. When you're traveling out of town, see if your friends can find someone, or try the Internet.

With paid sitters, you should make every effort to be a conscientious employer. Be timely, pay promptly, and call when you are unavoidably detained. With gratis sitters, like relatives and friends, encourage regular visits and make it easy for them—bring the child to their house, or leave a cooked meal for them if they're coming to your place. And remember, if you're balking at the expense of a paid baby-sitter, keep these wise words in mind.

> It's cheaper to spend the money on a baby-sitter and go out, even for an overnight in a hotel, than to get a divorce, no matter how little you think you make. Don't quit dating each other.

Spontaneity: Is It Gone for Good?

The answer is yes and no. Combustible spontaneous couplings can still be a key component in your sex life after the baby arrives, but now instead of seizing the perfect moment, you need to be ready to seize any available moment. Kids' naps and other short-term distractions provide opportunities to connect.

> When that baby goes down—GO INTO THE BEDROOM. Stop folding laundry, doing dishes whatever. My husband and I take turns dragging each other kicking and screaming into the bedroom— inevitably one of us is "too grumpy" or "tired." One helps the other get into it and we are always glad that we did!

> We have gotten into "quickies" when our child is preoccupied elsewhere. They are very short explosive sessions where quite a bit of our clothing stays on.

It's true that you don't have the luxury of waiting around till the mood strikes, but you may find that the novelty of tackling each other in unconventional times and places can really turn up the heat. You can also discreetly equip your house so that it's quickie-friendly: put condoms in several rooms, buy a quiet portable vibrator, and make sure there's lubricant stashed away. If baby sleeps in your room, and you live in anything bigger than a studio, you can designate a guest room or a corner of the living room for your trysts.

You will probably discover, however, that the demands of parenting greatly reduce the opportunities for spontaneous trysts. If you previously counted on having sex whenever the whim hit you, the constraints on your time and energy may short-circuit your libido.

> Sometimes my partner doesn't even want to have sex because we can't be spontaneous. He doesn't think it's fun because we don't have the limitless time to do lots of fun things like we used to.

There's no getting around the fact that once you're a parent, you can no longer enjoy sex that is both spontaneous and unrestricted. You are either going to have to cultivate your taste for quickies, or you are going to have to plan for sex. Many couples find this one of the most daunting barriers to resuming a sex life and assume that scheduling sex is bound to feel artificial and anti-erotic. But if you cast your mind back to just about every hot date you've ever had, you'll have to admit that a certain amount of premeditation was involved—perhaps you made reservations at a nice restaurant, dressed provocatively, rented an erotic movie, or purchased some new toys to try, all in preparation for an amorous exchange. Sure, being more forthright about your intentions means you can't pretend to be "swept off your feet," but you do get to enjoy the anticipation of a planned night of passion that can add an inspiring erotic tension to your day.

> We have designated Saturday as "sex night"—when we hang out all night together with a bottle of wine or margaritas after the kids go to bed. That's when we have the opportunity to get into more relaxed sex or multiple "episodes" if we want. Almost nothing is allowed to get in the way of our Saturday nights. During the day we tease each other about what's going to go on—knowing it's going to happen adds to the excitement, so that we're practically ripping each other's clothes off by the time the kids go to bed.

If the idea of "planning for sex" strikes you as rather clinical, with sex reduced to a routine physical exchange accompanied by the ticking of a clock, it's time to think outside the box. Your goal here is intimacy; how you define sex is up to you. For some it's a kiss, for others it's a bag of tricks.

We kiss a lot, say "I love you" a lot. I make an effort to kiss very consciously and deeply, and press my body hard against his. Usually it doesn't lead to anything, but once in a while, he'll kiss me a little harder, then I'll kiss him a little harder. We take it very slowly, step-by-step, so that if one of us isn't really into it, the other can easily back off with no hurt feelings.

Just the intimacy of a little make out session, a bit of oral sex, or a furtive hand job can help with the sense of "we've had some intimate time."

And just because your date is planned, doesn't mean the sex has to be.

My boyfriend and I have recently started using the book *101 Grrreat Quickies* and we are having a blast! So far all the treats have been something that can be done after the kids are in bed, but they are sufficiently unusual and fun that there's always a sense of surprise and anticipation—I wonder if he'll give me the coupon tonight or later in the week?!

Spending regular time together where you won't be interrupted by a needy child, where you can engage in adult conversation (preferably not about your child!), and where both parents can relax at the same time, will go a long way toward establishing a comfortable environment where your sexuality can begin to flourish. By scheduling time with your partner, you ensure that the relationship does not get buried beneath all the other obligations, you affirm his or her importance in your life, and you keep a grasp on your own identity as an adult, sexual woman.

How do you go about planning? The same way you plan for dinner, doctor's appointments, and vacations—by scheduling it on your calendars, datebooks, or palm pilots. Pick the best time each week, or choose the same time every week. Remember to keep it manageable, especially at first. The idea is to relax and reconnect with each other. It's important to be flexible and to communicate honestly, so that if one of you isn't feeling romantic, you can spend the time being intimate in other ways.

> We make a date for sex ahead of time, then, because it has been planned for, neither of us will get sidetracked by a book or the dishes. That way it's a little more special, and if we find that later we're not really into it, we can at least have that time together to talk or watch a video.

Spending recreational time together without the kids helps build intimacy. You don't need to be gazing deeply into each other's eyes and sharing all your hopes and dreams every week. Simply being alone with each other doing things you like to do will go a long way to reaffirming your connection. If you get tired of planning, you can buy season tickets to favorite events, take turns picking movies or restaurants, play board games at home, or go on walks together after work.

Privacy: A Little Lock Goes a Long Way

The freedom to make love wherever the mood strikes has always been regulated by standards of public decency, and you've probably limited your lovemaking to the confines of your home. Now, even that sanctuary is under assault from the curious eyes of your offspring. With kids around, you develop a keen appreciation for privacy, whether you're escaping a bed shared with a slumbering infant, minimizing the chances a jealous toddler will sabotage intimate moments, or sharing a house with a teen who's "grossed out" to think of parents "doing it."

> Kids seem to have an amazing sixth sense of when adults are about to do it— it can be frustrating. My teenage daughter complains bitterly every time I have sex. She bangs on the ceiling with a broom if she thinks we're making too much noise—and somehow she always knows!

Regardless of how much time you free up or whether you've moved mountains in order to spend the evening together, if you have no privacy, you won't be able to relax and enjoy the ride.

My children know that our bedroom is off-limits. It's our private space, and they respect that. We have a lock on the door, and we use it. This keeps me from worrying that they might walk in during sex, as I've found that anything at all that makes me inhibited is a bad thing for intimacy.

Assess your physical space
If you find that privacy is practically nonexistent in your house, we suggest checking to see if you can implement a few of these changes.

Get a lock on your bedroom door
This simple, inexpensive solution holds the key—literally—to your peace of mind. Perhaps our biggest collective anxiety when it comes to having sex is the fear that our kids will barge in on us mid-orgasm. While this is hardly going to irreparably traumatize your children (certainly not as much as the prospect seems to traumatize parents!), why worry about something that is so easy to prevent? Installing a lock gives you a perfect opportunity to explain the concept of privacy to your children, a concept that they will embrace with enthusiasm as they grow older (see the Healthy Sex, Happy Families chapter for more on the subject of privacy and disclosure).

> A closed door must be respected. Privacy and mom's needs need to be stressed.

Create privacy
If you live in a one-room apartment, you might want to hang a curtain or put up a screen to create a feeling of privacy. That way, when your child is absorbed in an activity alone you can be quietly affectionate without being visible.

Alternatives to the bedroom
Cramped living quarters necessitate a creative approach to lovemaking. You'd be surprised at the variety of alternatives moms have come up with.

> Once or twice we jumped into the shower while our child was engrossed in something else on the other side of the house.

> I have almost all my sex outside on the balcony.

> Activities like mutual masturbation, dry-humping, things that can be

done in a car, or the kitchen, under a blanket we do a good deal of, because it's quicker, and you don't have to explain why Mommy is on top of Daddy, or vice-versa.

Several mothers reported that one of the benefits of sharing a "family bed" (see below), was that it forced them to have sex outside the bedroom, which infused their sex lives with a greater sense of adventure.

I found that having sex in the living room or office right after I nurse her to sleep for the night (that way I know she is sound asleep and won't wake for at least two hours) has the right touch of sneakiness, spontaneity, and feels a bit naughty.

Hot Tips: Privacy Enhancers

Don't let a nosy kid stop you from enjoying sex. Privacy simply requires creativity and spontaneity:

- Put a lock on the bedroom door
- Reconsider family bed
- Enforce bed time
- Keep a guest room stocked with lube and sex toys
- Try quickies in the shower
- Try sex outdoors on the balcony or in the backyard
- Have a tryst while the kids are watching cartoons

We set aside our guest room as our "playroom" for a while and would retreat there as our "getaway right at home." I mean just a candle, some body lotion, a "toy" or two stashed in there and we were in the mood.

Assess your habits
You might also need to change your style in order to ensure privacy.

Tone it down
Lovemaking that involves screaming and moaning can be understandably

confusing and frightening to a child. Lower the audio if you can do so without dampening your enthusiasm. Otherwise, consider soundproofing your room by putting carpeting on the floors or investing in some insulation. If your bed springs are squeaky, put the mattress on the floor, get a new mattress, or try a futon. If your room is next to your child's, have sex somewhere else in the house. Use quiet sex toys like the hand-held electric vibrators that resemble hair brushes, or use them under the covers so the fabric muffles the sound.

Think twice about family bed

If your baby sleeps with you in a "family bed," you need to be realistic about the impact this will have on your sex life. Family bed, also known as "cosleeping," refers to the practice of letting a child (or children) sleep in the same bed as their parents. Advocates of family bed maintain that this practice strengthens the bond between parent and child. Many parents actively choose this practice, while others fall into it during their child's infancy either because nighttime breastfeeding is easier with the baby close by, or because baby falls asleep in the bed while nursing.

While we don't doubt that family bed benefits children, it does exact a price on adults. You are sharing your most intimate space with your child, and unless you make a conscious effort to create other opportunities to be alone together, the effect is to demote your adult relationship to second string. This can lead to a sense of neglect, resentment, and ultimately no sex. If you're single, family bed may be even harder to resist, since your child fills a need for closeness and physical contact. In either case, should you want to reclaim your bed at some point for yourself and/or a partner, evicting the child will be no picnic. During infancy, family bed may be the only way to maximize your sleep, but we recommend teaching your child how to sleep alone as soon as you can.

Those who practice family bed have mixed reactions about its effect on their sex lives. Some find it rejuvenating, since it forced them out of a sex-in-the-bedroom rut.

> Our third child is cosleeping with us and I have found that has revitalized our sex life and knocked us out of the nighttime, bedroom sex routine we'd fallen into. We're challenged to find new places and new times.

Others, like this mom, find that the baby's proximity interferes with sex in practical as well as psychological ways.

It's been hard to have a sex life for a lot of reasons. Part of it is that we have a family bed, and the baby wakes up any time we start to have sex. I'm not comfortable having intercourse when I've got the baby on one arm, nursing or whatever.

The most sensitive issue family bed raises is whether or not it's appropriate for parents to have sex with a baby in the bed. Culturally, we are schooled to keep our kids and our sex lives separate, so most people treat the prospect of children being in the presence of any adult sexual activity as a violation of the most primal taboo. But a sleeping baby is oblivious to its environment, so if your hanky-panky won't disturb his or her slumbers, we say have at it.

Sex and motherhood don't really mix well in the public imagination. For example, when I read in this really popular parenting book that sex with your infant in bed was disgusting and deplorable, I thought, okay the baby in bed during sex is unacceptable and perverse. But the fact of the matter is we don't have that many opportunities to make love. And if the baby is sleeping in bed with us, we are not going to risk waking him up by moving him to his room. It takes a bit of reckoning to be your own person, rather than a mother who toes the mainstream, conservative line.

Bear in mind that in other cultures where space and privacy are not options, kids of all ages sleep in the same room with parents (who presumably continue to have sex). In fact, 90% of parents around the world sleep with their children in the same room. But those of us who are products of American culture are distinctly inhibited by the prospect of our children seeing or hearing our lovemaking. Most parents practicing family bed will choose to have sex in other rooms once their kids pass infancy. In the end, as the following moms attest, it's all about exploring your own personal "comfort zone."

Even sharing the hotel rooms on vacation never really stopped us. Our daughter just said we kissed loud.

You have to explore your comfort zones regarding sexuality and your children. My partner and I felt comfortable making love in spoons position while our baby slept next to me. Now that our children are older, we simply tell them that we are having some alone time. They know EXACTLY what that means (they like to giggle when we say that), and have learned to knock before they burst through our closed bedroom door.

Level with your kid

Although the previous suggestions are geared toward minimizing kids' awareness of your activities, it will not kill them if they know what you're up to. Which is to say, don't freak out if they catch you in the act. And don't obsess over keeping them in the dark. By being honest with your children, you send the message that sex is natural, healthy, and nothing to be ashamed of. You can teach your children to respect your private time, and answer their questions in an age-appropriate way as they arise.

> I think it's okay for children to see their parents being sexual. I mean you want to be prudent and respectful but if they see a healthy sex life in their home they will better be able to filter through all the hang-ups our society has about sexuality and hopefully recognize the unhealthy, belittling, exploitative, and controlling portrayals of sex out there in our media and society.

> I grew up in a house where I could hear my parents having sex. I didn't know what they were doing, but I don't think most children jump to a conclusion that something bad is happening. I think it's a healthy household noise! Children should be accustomed to it and raised in an atmosphere where this kind of expression is understood as healthy. And of course, they should be encouraged to ask questions . . . even the hard ones!

Energy: When Power Bars Are Not Enough

Women are told that the physical exertion required for childbirth equals that of running a marathon. We'll take it one step further and contend that raising children is the physical equivalent of participating in a decathlon—one with no finish line! First event: childbirth. Second event: breastfeeding. Third event: sleep deprivation. Fourth event: day care. Fifth event: back to work. Sixth event: housekeeping . . . You get the picture. Nonbiological moms may skip the first two events, but they have to hit the ground running once their child arrives. It's no wonder so many women complain that they've lost their libidos—they're too busy running the race to look for them.

Since sex requires a certain amount of energy, it's not surprising that overextended parents might find themselves preferring sleep or a quiet meal over a roll in the hay.

> I find that the thought of sex can often make me even more tired.
> However actually having sex can boost my energy level for weeks.
> So, as weird as it sounds, as an unpartnered single mom, I try to
> make sure that I have sex at somewhat regular intervals.

As this mom notes, the beauty of sex is that it actually rejuvenates you—replenishing mind, body, and spirit. So if you find that you're too tired for sex, too worn out to masturbate, or too stressed out to fantasize, we urge you to examine a few of the following ways to boost your energy. (See the Fanning the Flames of Desire chapter for tips on what to do when your sex drive takes an extended vacation.)

Exercise

Make exercise a part of your daily routine and you will experience a noticeable change in your energy level. The endorphins released during exercise improve your mood and give your libido a lift. Your self-esteem surges because you're doing something just for yourself, and you're getting back into shape. Go on regular stroller walks, join an aerobics class, sign up for yoga.

Eat well

Whatever you do, don't skip meals. Unfortunately, some new mothers are so horrified that their bodies don't magically snap back into shape after childbirth that they diet compulsively. If you're breastfeeding, you need to eat regularly and nutritiously both for your sake and the baby's. If you're not breastfeeding and you want to diet, just make sure you're eating well-balanced meals. A power bar might be great for a midday energy boost, but subsisting on them will leave you run down.

Sleep

Who wants to have sex when you can SLEEP!?

When you've got to have it, nothing else will do. With infants, try to sleep when they do. Get your partner to take the night shift or have a friend or relative sleep over a few nights so you can rest. With older kids, try to go to bed earlier. Take catnaps during your lunch break. Skip chores, cancel appointments, call in sick—whatever it takes—if it means you can catch up on some sleep.

Get out of the house

Escaping your routine can go a long way toward boosting your energy level. Whether it's going for a walk, having coffee with a friend, or planning an overnight getaway, just removing yourself from an environment that revolves around children can help you feel less like a mom, and more like a woman.

> An annual parents-only vacation has made a huge difference for us. Even after we come home, a bit of that romance lingers for us because we actively create it. On vacation we buy music or art or clothes that we can see and touch and hear to remind us of those intimate days alone.

Do things alone

As much as possible, try to arrange regular chunks of time to be by yourself. This allows you to step outside your role as mom, and take a break from the demands on your time and attention. Trade breaks with your partner or hire a sitter, but make this a priority. Set aside time to read your favorite magazine or newspaper, visit a museum, go to the gym or the movies, but spend time on yourself.

Get help with household chores

Despite the fact that vast numbers of women now also work outside the home, they still do the bulk of the child care and housekeeping.[1] Needless to say, this can lead to resentment within relationships unless you figure out a way to split the duties or compensate for the inequity. Many women cited frustration with domestic issues as a cause of diminished desire—see the Chore Wars sidebar for some practical tips on combating the issue.

We fuss more about household responsibilities and that leads to anger that sometimes affects my desire for sex. I can't feel very sexy if I've spent all day cleaning up after a grown man who puts forth little or no effort to help and that leads to resentment and decreased energy which leaves him out of luck sometimes. After all these years, that's the biggest battleground for us.

Keep an open mind

With all the demnds of motherhood, it's hard to avoid slipping into the "we're too tired/busy/tense to have sex" mode. But sexual pleasure can be relaxing in and of itself, and often moms find that simply being receptive to the idea leads to encounters that replenish body and soul. This mom finds that one of the benefits of planned sex is that it gives her an opportunity to get in the mood.

I find I need some adjustment time between going from "mom" to "lover," and he gives me that time, even if it's just a half hour soak in a bubble bath between putting the kids to bed and starting our evening together. That time helps me adjust, lets me relax, and gives me a few minutes for a new headspace to kick in.

Hot Tips: Chore Wars

Chores were bad enough before the kid, but now your little bundle of love makes twice as much work for you; you feel stuck in an endless cycle of picking up toys, doing laundry, and cleaning up food disasters. By their very nature, chores are unpleasant—they're time-consuming, tiring and monotonous. It's easy to resent the amount of time and energy you spend on them—who wouldn't rather be lying poolside with a cold drink in her hand rather than vacuuming up the day's cookie crumbs? This resentment can sour a relationship, but with a little planning you can avoid waging World War III over the mashed carrots on the carpet.

- Itemize the chores. Make a list of the chores, including child care and parenting activities. Keep track of the duties performed by each of you during an

---

average week (or month) and write down how long each one takes. Use this as a starting point to discuss a redistribution of work. If your partner is relatively oblivious to his or her domestic comforts, it may help to see—quantifiably—how much time is involved in upkeep.

- Assess your standards and goals. How clean does your house really have to be? Oh, we know it's hard to give up a tidy house, but if you're the only one that really cares about a spotless toilet bowl and smudge-free mirrors, maybe it's time to lower your standards a teensy bit. Clean the house once a month instead of once a week. Pick up the toys on the weekend instead of every evening.

- Agree on your split. Do you want to divide up the chores 50/50 or use a different ratio? Be attentive when assigning a higher share to stay-at-home moms. She may not be punching a clock, but the care, feeding, and teaching of children is definitely hard work. If you agree in principle that the chores should be split equally, but one of you doesn't have enough time, consider letting her or him pay for a housecleaner or a baby-sitter.

- Compromise. To minimize the drudgery, divide up the chores according to what suits each of you best. Choose chores which match your skills or interests and they won't seem as much like work. If you both like the same things, take turns choosing a chore from the list, or you can alternate your duties from month to month.

- Schedule time to do the chores.. Don't assume they'll take care of themselves, or Sunday nights will be hell in your house—the kids will be whining about going to school as you whine about the laundry. Make a schedule and keep to it, but give yourself the day off once in a while!

- Negotiate. If you can't do your chores, negotiate some alternative solution rather than just blowing them off. Bribe a kid to do them (don't make a habit of it), or swap with your partner: "If you do the laundry today, I'll make dinner tomorrow."

- Don't criticize. Everyone has their own style, so don't disparage your partner's efforts by complaining about the work. If you don't like the artful design vacuumed into the rug, keep your mouth shut! At least the darn thing is clean, so why not just compliment your partner on his or her unique domestic aesthetic?

- Be flexible. If one of you misses a chore, don't panic. There are more important things in life than housework, so allow for higher priorities. And give yourselves the weekend off once in a while so you don't miss out on more enjoyable pursuits.

- Get help. You don't have to do it all yourselves. Teach your kids how to pick up their toys, make their beds, and help out around the house when they're old enough. Hire professionals if you can afford it or avail yourself of some time-saving alternatives (on-line shopping, a dishwasher, diaper service, etc.).
- Reward yourselves. Make rewards part of your routine, whether it's treating yourselves to a night out, taking turns with massage, or playing hooky from your chores once in a while!

Others simply accept fatigue as part of parenthood, and discover ways to balance their sexual needs with their bodies' demands.

> We make an assumption: great sex means we're going to be tired the next day, no question about it. If the sex is good enough, it's worth it, so we don't bother having lackluster sex now. And it's not like we're not tired all the time, anyway! We have small children!

> Being tired is the main difference. I have learned to work with it. There is rarely a time when I'm not tired, so even though I may not want it right at the same moment my partner does I always give him a chance to "convince" me. I have to say he is usually successful at convincing me. I have yet to regret his advances.

Saying No to Supermom

Inevitably, women take on a somewhat daunting sense of responsibility when they become moms. Because mothers are still considered the primary caretakers for children, they shoulder the blame for everything that is less than perfect in this new being's life. Of course every mom we know is also holding down a job and managing day-to-day household responsibilities. Instead of addressing the inequities of what's been called a mother's "second shift" with societal solutions such as subsidized childcare or mandatory flexible work schedules for both male and female parents, our society has come up with the ridiculous ideal of Supermom. You know Supermom. She doesn't see any reason to change society because she can juggle two or three shifts and never break a sweat. She's white, middle-class, well-educated, and somehow manages to raise attractive and well-behaved children according to the latest received wisdom on parenting, all while holding down a successful corporate job. Did we mention that she has retained her girlish figure and that you'll find her on many nights sharing a gourmet dinner with her husband over candlelight and cell phones, the kids tucked safely in bed?

Supermom is a complete nightmare of a role model, and we say—wake up! The pressure to live up to the ideal is killing us. In our efforts to be good moms, good partners, and generally likable people, we make a lot of sacrifices. We shouldn't have to work so hard to get access to the simple things—time, privacy, sexual pleasure—that renew and replenish us. Child care should be subsidized, baby-sitters bountiful, partners understanding, and children cooperative. But this is usually not the case, so we tend to compensate by protecting our children's quality of life at the expense of our own. But don't you deserve to live the kind of pleasure-filled life you want your kids to grow up and have? After all, how are your sons and daughters going to avoid the trap of impossible ideals themselves if you don't show them how to trust their own experience? We invite you NOT to be Supermom. Let something go. Do for yourself. Be selfish. So what if you can't leap tall buildings in a single bound? You will love yourself, and from there all good things will come.

7

Fanning the Flames
of Desire

For many of us, sexual desire is the barometer by which to measure both our health and well-being, and our compatibility with a partner. An absence of sexual desire, no matter how brief, tends to fill us with fear. When our libido takes a dive, we assume it will never resurface. When our sex life becomes bland, or our sexual encounters become fewer and farther between, we begin to wonder if our relationships are doomed.

> I get "upset" if I'm not getting turned on like I want to. I feel like something is wrong with me.

In the Sometimes You're Hot, Sometimes You're Not chapter we examined a variety of factors that can affect your sex drive and encouraged you to accept fluctuations over your lifetime as natural and inevitable. However, even a supremely self-accepting woman is bound to find this attitude hard to sustain once she's negotiating the ebb and flow of libido with a partner. Trying to harmonize your sexual desires with someone else's can quickly deteriorate into a game of cat and mouse, rife with frustration, missed opportunities, misunderstandings, and petty cruelties. But you can change the rules of the game, and the first rule to go should be the notion that diminished desire signifies a failed relationship. On the contrary, as psychotherapist Jack Morin points out in his book *The Erotic Mind,* "Experts blame waning passion on lack of communication, lack of intimacy, trust, etc. But good relationships don't automatically lead to good sex. Often in the best relationships passion becomes elusive."[1] In this chapter we'll take a closer look at why passion disappears, suggest ways to get it back, and show you how to keep your perspective.

Expectations and Realities

While much of the material in this chapter is applicable to both single and partnered moms, it's of particular relevance to couples in long-term relationships. For reasons we discuss below in the Nostalgia section, waning desire is seldom an issue in the early stages of a relationship. But if you've been with the same partner for more than two years, you probably already know how difficult it is to stay in tune sexually. If you've read any sex manuals or discussed this subject with a therapist, you may recognize several clinical terms. "Desire disorder" or "desire dysfunction" are the umbrella terms for ongoing difficulties achieving arousal or orgasm. When couples are dealing with libidos that aren't in synch, they're described as having a "desire discrepancy." And the colloquial term for a couple's mutual, ongoing disinterest in sex is "bed death." While all of these terms have an ominous or downright pathologizing ring to them, they actually describe perfectly healthy situations that are common to a large portion of the population. The fact that your sex drive has headed south, that your partner doesn't seem remotely interested in sex, or that neither of you seem to be in synch at the same time does not indicate that there's anything wrong with either one of you. Desire issues usually result from the fact that your realities don't match your expectations. If you cultivate more realistic expectations, you can learn to appreciate your own desires, wherever they may wander.

Good sex takes work

As the entertainer Bette Midler once quipped, "If sex is such a natural phenomenon, how come there are so many how-to books?" Few enough people in our society receive accurate information about the biological basics of sex, and practically no one receives accurate information about the emotional complexities of sex. In an age touted for its scientific discoveries, technological advancements, and communications revolution, we still aren't providing accurate sex education in schools, homes, or medical settings. Instead, the media substitutes as our instructor. Disney teaches kids that one kiss will solve all life's problems; movies and glossy magazines dish up airbrushed, blissed-out, celebrity unions; and the advertising industry assures us that only the young and beautiful deserve to get laid.

Nobody ever tells or shows us that a satisfying sex life requires work. Psychologist Lenore Tiefer points out that there's no bridge between our own experience (or lack of experience) and our cultural expectations.

> Imagine how you would feel if playing gin rummy, and playing it well, were considered a major component of happiness and a major sign of maturity, but no one told you how to play, you never saw anyone else play, and everything you ever read implied that normal and healthy people just somehow "know" how to play and really enjoy playing the very first time they try! It is a very strange situation.[2]

When sexual relationships show any sign of faltering, we start by worrying, move on to pointing fingers, then we panic, and oftentimes we flee. But sexual fulfillment requires just as much information-gathering, communication, and persistence as parenting does. A new sexual partner won't know how to please you for the first time without your explicit feedback, and a long-term partner won't know how to please you for the one-thousandth time without your explicit feedback (trust us, your feedback will have changed). Self-awareness is crucial, and it does take effort to get to know yourself: from your sexual anatomy and responses, to your hormonal fluctuations, to your deepest erotic desires and fantasies. Ultimately, only you can teach yourself how to have good sex, because only you know how you define good sex. And defining your terms is an ongoing process—one that changes throughout your life.

Challenges for the new mom
The logistical challenges of parenting (see the Having It All chapter) are a piece of cake compared to the emotional and physical challenges that make you and your partners so susceptible to a decreased sex drive while your kids are young. Sure, plenty of women gain a sense of power and accomplishment from becoming mothers that ultimately boosts their sexual energy. But it's a safe bet you'll experience a decline in libido and a corresponding decline in sexual activity during the first year or two of your child's life. Or, as a typical survey respondent put it:

Sex? What is this "sex" of which you speak? I've heard of it, but for the life of me I can't remember what it is.

This lowered libido may or may not trouble you and your partners. Some women are perfectly blithe about their shift in focus, and many parents are self-possessed enough to take the long view.

I have absolutely zero libido. Just want to nibble on the baby's plump sweet body. Can't even feel aroused at the site of a handsome movie devil's triceps.

I just don't sweat it. I'm in my marriage for the long haul, so short-term lapses in romance (and I consider a year or two to be short-term) are no big deal. My husband agrees.

Following childbirth, a biological mother's libido may be hit with the impact of physical recovery, fatigue, changing self-image, changing priorities, and postpartum depression. The following common sources of stress affect biological and nonbiological parents alike and offer ample reason to cultivate compassion for yourself and your partners.

Hormones

The impact of hormonal changes on a biological mother's libido can't be underestimated. Many of our survey respondents commented that they had no warning that a postpartum drop in estrogen and the rise in prolactin accompanying breastfeeding would have such a sexually depressive effect. As one mom put it:

Let women know that desire does return. I thought my pussy had died after three births in three years, accompanied by seven years of nursing, but it has made quite a comeback.

But biological mothers aren't the only parents affected by hormonal shifts—which may explain why they aren't the only parents who can experience an increase in prolactin levels (probably as a result of bonding) and a decrease in testosterone levels (probably as a result of stress). Presumably nonbiological moms would have the same experience. Lowered testosterone levels can result in a lowered libido in both men and women.

Guilt

It's not unusual for new parents, especially moms, to become completely wrapped up in care taking and to feel guilty if their focus wavers for an instant. If you perceive sexual pleasure as at best a frivolity, and at worst a dangerous distraction from the more important task at hand, you won't be particularly motivated to be sexual.

> My sex life changed dramatically because I went from being self-focused to being child-focused. I spent much less time on my own pursuits.

> Initially I couldn't fathom having sex. It was a total cognitive dissonance for me. It took many months (and I'm still working on it!) before I didn't feel guilty having sex. I believed I should be totally focused on my daughter, even when she was sleeping. Sex took me away from her, and at times I was anxious something awful would happen to her while we were having sex.

One of your greatest challenges as a mother will be walking the line between selflessness and selfishness. Part of a healthy selfishness is recognizing that kids can't—and shouldn't be expected to—fulfill your needs for emotional and sexual intimacy. Prioritizing your adult relationships helps you to be a better mother as well as a happier woman. Of course, as we'll discuss later in this chapter, adult relationships do present challenges that the relatively straightforward relationship of mother and baby does not.

> Parents should put themselves first, put their relationship on the front burner. That took awhile to sink in—realizing that we can't be good parents if we are not a good couple and partnership. Sometimes it is harder to be a wife than a mom.

Loss of self

Becoming a mother can present a serious identity crisis, since in our culture it can result in what anthropologist Sheila Kitzinger refers to as a "virtual annihilation of self." While increased status has typically accompanied a woman's transition to motherhood at other times and in other cultures, here's how she describes the effects of this transition in the Western world:

When a woman turns into a mother she is treated suddenly as less, not more. She tends to be perceived by men, and by other women who are not themselves mothers, as having fewer skills, and reduced competence, intellectual capacity, and commitment to the things that matter. Her identity has become that of "a mother," and it is as if the rest of her—her working skills, her career goals, and all her other interests—has vanished.[3]

Maintaining your own identity is not only essential to your mental health, it's vital to the health of your relationships. Without a strong sense of self you won't necessarily feel entitled to your own desires.

I think that I have in some ways become shy about addressing my own wants and needs and that sometimes I play the mother role as an unhealthy buffer to avoid dealing with the issues I do have about safety and trust. I hide out in my motherhood.

On a practical level, you may well feel like you don't have time or space for your own desires. Caring for children, especially infants, is both incredibly demanding and incredibly gratifying, so it's not surprising if everything and everyone else in your life recedes into the background upon their arrival. You may resent this narrowing of your horizons, or you may delight in a sense of higher purpose.

Having a baby and integrating her into my life has been emotionally and physically draining. It is like my brain cannot fit any need other than the baby, so it is very difficult to find the energy even to give my partner a hug when he needs it.

I'm fulfilled by my child so sex isn't as important anymore.

Mothers are expected and encouraged to put all their energies into bonding with their babies. The current philosophy of "attachment parenting" is based on perfectly sound ideas about the importance of providing infants with consistent, attentive care, but in time-honored tradition it places the ultimate responsibility for this care on mothers.[4] (Parenting trends may come and go, but Mom is invariably left holding the bag.) If you spend your days in constant contact with an infant, you're more likely to spend your nights dreaming about getting a little personal space than getting a little action.

> Not only is my sex drive just about gone, but practicing attachment parenting makes having sex nearly impossible. My son sleeps in our bed and sleeps the exact hours we do, so there is literally no time for sex. Plus, I hold him so much during the day that I am touched out by the end of the day. I just want to be left alone at night.

The intimacy you have with an infant may feel so all-encompassing that it's difficult to make room for any other feelings.

> I felt almost a chemical change, where sex becomes completely secondary and my entire affection was directly toward my child. I wanted to give all my physical love to my child. It freaked me out a little at first, but I was so in love with my child it really didn't matter. And in the end, as your child grows, you regain your sense of your self and your sexual self.

As the survey respondent above suggests, the infatuation phase with your infant will wear off, and your old familiar yearnings and appetites will come flooding back to you. We all know that motherhood has a lot to teach us about self-sacrifice and nurturing, but no one ever points out that spending time with an infant has a lot to teach us about the integrity of human desires. If you can learn to apply the same attention, respect, and acceptance to your own desires as you do to your child's, you'll be well-equipped to enjoy being both a good mother and a satisfied lover.

> Becoming a mom has caused me to become MUCH more aware of myself as a sexual being. I feel much more in touch with my body, and I have no embarrassment any more about masturbating, experiencing sexual pleasure, or trying new things.

Challenges for the relationship

Becoming parents presents a huge challenge to even the strongest relationships. Statistics show that marital satisfaction plummets during the first two years of parenting, an occurrence which takes most parents by surprise.[5] As Harriet Lerner, psychotherapist and author of *The Mother Dance,* explains, "Nothing is more stressful than the addition or subtraction of family members. We understand the subtraction part, because loss is the most difficult adaptational task we deal with. But we underestimate the incredible stress of adding a new family member to the system." An appreciation for the magni-

tude of your adjustment can help you keep your perspective. "Don't expect
to have a sex life during the first two years after the child's birth," advises
Lerner. "If it happens, consider it to be an 'extra.' But reduce your expectations
to zero because a new baby is a crisis of enormous proportions in the life of
a couple, and especially the mother from whom more is expected."

> I'm happy having less sex right now. However, I'm unhappy with
> the perception that I must have some problem if my sex drive is
> low. It seems perfectly normal to me that people who have averaged
> three to four sleep interruptions per night over an eight month
> period, plus hauling a heavy child around all day, have less need for
> sex than other creature comforts.

Whatever conflicts you may have had in your relationship prior to having children will only be amplified by their arrival. Most new parents consis-
tently fight about the same things: money, child care, housework, careers,
social life, and sex.[6] Although both partners are dealing with the demands of
parenting, heterosexual women typically bear the greater burden because the
division of labor tends to break down along traditional gender lines (studies
do show that lesbian parents share childcare tasks more equally than heterosexual parents).[7] In other words, mothers with male partners end up doing
more household chores, assuming primary responsibility for child care, sac-
rificing or postponing a career, etc. One typical survey respondent describes
this scenario:

> I all of a sudden became the mom of two instead of one. Once we
> decided that it was best if I was the one to stay home, I acquired a
> full-grown child who sees me as a mom, not as his wife anymore.

It's hardly surprising that studies show wives often experience greater
marital dissatisfaction than husbands, which researchers suggest has to do with
the gap between their optimistic expectations and the harsh realities of domestic life.[8] You don't need to be a rocket scientist or a sex therapist to figure out
how this frustrating state of affairs could negatively impact your sex life.

> Find a partner who contributes fully in terms of childcare and
> household duties—it is impossible to feel sexual if you're the one
> getting up three times a night to take care of your newborn while
> the other snores away.

Preparation, communication, and compromise will be your biggest allies in achieving domestic harmony. Face it, both you and your partner are dealing with the same stressors, even if it sometimes feels like you're each the primary source of the other's stress. Domestic stress frequently decreases sexual desire, but if you work together to create coping mechanisms, you'll be laying the groundwork for rediscovering your erotic interest in each other. Once you make a decision regarding the division of labor, maintain an ongoing dialogue about how the arrangement is working. Keep partners apprised of how stress affects your sex drive, and what they can do to help.

> I need nonsexual attention—help with the babies, the housework, time to relax by myself (Calgon, take me away!), because without it, sex becomes a chore—just one more thing I have to do before I can get some sleep.

The bottom line is that you have to communicate about difficult or highly charged topics in order to keep your relationship vital—or even remotely interesting! If you keep a mental list of all your partner's perceived failures, but never articulate your distress, the resulting hostility will eat away at your sex drive. If you feel resentful about giving up your career, but never share this with a partner, you'll never have the chance to explore possible alternatives. If you're the partner of a new mom and feel jealous of, or excluded by, the mother/child bond, you'll only distance yourself further by staying silent. Of course, revealing your most petty emotions is risky, but risk is the very element you might need to reinvigorate your relationship. Certainly it is the very element that will bring sexual tension and erotic excitement back into the mix.

Defining your own terms

> I was never too tired for sex, but my ex had a very low sex drive, which was the problem. I think that people who are highly sexed will find the time and place. For others, having children is an excuse to give it up or reduce the frequency.

> I don't like the assumption that you have to prioritize having sex. I think there are phases of life where sex is more and less important, and it's fine if I'm taking a bit of a break right now.

Not enough is written or said about total loss of libido, and I am sure it is a very common experience. So much of what we read is about how to find time to have sex as if we are all just chock-full of desire and the one problem is finding time. But I avoid contact with my husband because I am not interested in sex.

Few topics seem to elicit quite so many judgments or so much defensiveness as defining an appropriate level of sexual desire, particularly in relation to a partner's: How much is too much? How much is too little? Will the real sick ticket in this relationship please stand up? The truth is, of course, that we're all entitled to enjoy as much or as little desire as we please. Although the focus of this chapter is on keeping the sexual flame burning in your relationships, we don't mean to imply that a relationship is only meaningful if you're sexually active together. As the survey respondent below points out, just because you're not "doing it" doesn't mean you lack an erotic connection.

Hot Tips: A Word about Communication

It's not enough to identify what inhibits or inspires your sex drive, you have to be able to articulate what you know and need to a partner. The following techniques are discussed in greater detail in the Talking to Your Partner About Sex Chapter, but we summarize them here since they'll be helpful to you during your discussions of desire.

- Make time to discuss sex.
- Avoid the heat of the moment.
- Be direct and clear, use specific examples.
- Avoid the negative.
- Don't make demands, make requests.
- Use I statements.
- Be an empathetic listener.
- Negotiate and compromise.
- Know when to stop talking.

I actually had a consensually celibate relationship for about five months when my son was three. We did a lot of thinking about how sex would impact each of us, our differing beliefs about abortion, my need for true intimacy, his fears about "entrapment," and we decided we would stop having sex, after one time. One VERY hot time. It was difficult but I learned more about my sexuality in that time than I learned in all the years before! I felt truly listened to, was tenderly touched, enjoyed great kissing, and we even slept together occasionally.

Plenty of parents are philosophical about the fact that it's difficult to keep sexual passion high on the agenda when there's a small child in the house.

We share love, compromise, friendship, and the realization that the sexual part of any relationship goes through ups and downs. It helps to know that we won't have a one-year-old forever, and that some-day down the road, we can just let her go out and play while we go upstairs and play!

Indeed, it's vital to recognize that your passions need not be continuously stoked to a white-heat intensity for you to qualify as a sexual being. You should certainly toss out the calendar rather than fretting over how many times this month you have or haven't had some kind of erotic encounter. Your sexual self-worth does not hinge on how often you do or don't have orgasms. This said, we're suspicious of women who proclaim that sex no longer matters to them because they're busy with the more meaningful task of mothering, and we have very limited tolerance for partners who become unable to view mothers as sexual creatures. We all live in a culture where sexual expression is viewed as a frivolous luxury and where mothers are expected to thrive on self-sacrifice. It's not always easy to distinguish between the social pressures herding your libido onto the back-burner and your own natural ebb and flow of desire. Rather than redefining yourself as a sexless, maternal being, you might find it helpful to redefine what being sexual means to you. As Susie Bright put it during a panel discussion on sex and parenting:

I don't have to be "doing it" every day, minute, or week to prove I have a sexual life. If you think of your sex life as something that's just tick, tick, ticking like a heart beat and you pay attention and recognize what affects that—that you have fantasies and daydreams—then your life is filled with sex. You're sensually aware that sex is part of being alive, and if you're feeling alive then you're having a sex life.

Roadblocks

If your sex drive, or your partner's, appears to have vanished without a trace, you are not alone. Our collective yearning for sustained passion keeps the mental health professionals in business and fuels a million-dollar industry of self-help books. Books such as *Hot Monogamy*, *The Erotic Mind*, and *I'm Not in the Mood* all attempt to unlock the complex mysteries of sexual desire, while instruction manuals such as *101 Nights of Great Sex* promise instant gratification. We consumers eat them up in the hopes that we'll learn how to time-travel back to that magical honeymoon stage of our relationship.

In fact, there are no time machines, effective aphrodisiacs, or money-back guarantees. The only fundamental truth is that your sexuality is unique: techniques that enhance desire for one person might leave you indifferent, and vice-versa. Your emotions, your sexual history, your values, and your physiology all influence what arouses you. Add your partner's own particular sexual profile, throw in a variety of external factors related to your relationship, and you've got a chemistry that's exclusive to the two of you.

This is not to say that many couples don't stumble over the same obstacles or pass through some of the same phases in their relationships—they do. But you're more likely to overcome a problem—sexual or nonsexual—if you understand all the contributing factors. To that end, we invite you to examine how the following common roadblocks to sexual satisfaction might apply to your own situation.

Expectations

Many of us suffer from the unrealistic expectation that sexual partners should be perfectly in tune and perfectly sufficient to satisfy each other's desires. We find it threatening to experience different degrees of desire, to experience desire at different times, or to experience desire for different things. While we are hardly likely to take it as a personal affront if our partner feels like going for a jog or eating some ice cream when we don't, we tend to feel anxious, guilty, or irritated if our partner has sexual desires we don't share.

Few differences feel quite as threatening to a relationship as a discrepancy in sex drive. Since we equate sexual desire with love and attraction, we tend to leap to the conclusion: "If you don't want to have sex with me, you must not love me." The truth is that sex drives simply differ from individual to individual. Or as Pat Love, psychotherapist and author of *Hot Monogamy,* comments, "some degree of desire discrepancy seems to be the human condition."[9] As we discussed in the Sometimes You're Hot... Chapter, there does seem to be a hormonal component to this naturally occurring discrepancy. Studies suggest that testosterone levels influence libido, and that individuals with higher levels of naturally occurring testosterone, or so-called "high-T" individuals, will have higher sex drives. While men, by definition, have much higher levels of testosterone than women, some researchers speculate that women compensate for this discrepancy by having a higher sensitivity to testosterone, so that a little goes a long way.

Couples experiencing desire discrepancies may find it helpful to learn that their differences could have a biochemical component. When libido is conceived as something that fluctuates innately, rather than as something that "should" be at a certain "normal" level in a "healthy, loving" relationship, the desire discrepancy loses much of its negative charge. The low desire partner is released from feelings of inadequacy and guilt, and the high desire partner from feelings of failure or rejection.

Of course, it does you no good to identify a desire gap if you're not also willing to strategize ways to bridge it (see the "Let's Make a Deal" sidebar for some tips.) Rather than focusing on which of you seems to be "high-T" or "low-T," you and your partner may find it helpful to get to know your respective body rhythms in order to make the most of individual highs and lows. Some women notice a distinct increase in libido at different times of their menstrual cycle—such as mid-cycle when estrogen levels are higher. Some individuals notice a distinct increase in libido at different times of day—such as in the morning, when testosterone levels are higher.

> My husband knows that my monthly cycle provides me with about
> a week of feeling romantic, a week of lust, a week of slowing down,
> and a week of no desire. We work around that.

It can be useful and fun to play biology professor when it comes to mapping out your sex drives, but needless to say, there's a lot more to desire than biology. Plenty of emotional and environmental factors also come into play. Sometimes simply feeling freed from the pressure of a partner's expectations is enough to rekindle libido.

> The partner CANNOT take it personally when the mother is too
> tired or freaked to be sexual. Sometimes my desire came back sim-
> ply because my husband said I didn't have to have sex.

Another common discrepancy that can jeopardize a couple's sense of sexual compatibility is a simple difference in what sex means to each partner. We're motivated to have sex for a variety of reasons: physical release, sensual closeness, emotional connection, ego-gratification, and more. Our differences only become problematic if we think our partner's motivation is somehow not as legitimate as our own.

> The emotional and spiritual element of sex has become more and more important to me since having children, and my husband hasn't understood that at all. Sex is still a completely physical experience for him, and I wish it could deepen.

> My husband has always equated love with sex and it took him some time to see that I could love him without always making love to him.

If you can let go of the expectation that sex should mean the same thing to both of you, and communicate honestly about your own motivation, you'll be more likely to get what you want out of your sexual encounters.

Nostalgia

Part of the reason so many couples in long-term relationships struggle with the gap between expectations and reality is that early in their relationship, expectations and reality seemed to be in perfect synch. You probably have fond memories of the heady early days of your love affair: you couldn't keep your hands off each other; the simple touch of your lover's hand was enough to make your entire body tingle with arousal; you were willing to be more sexually adventurous; and you could stay up half the night making love and wake up raring to get right back down to action. Remember how intoxicating it all felt? That's because you were intoxicated—there's considerable evidence that during the initial euphoria of a love affair we're under the influence of an amphetamine-like brain chemical known as PEA. What is sometimes referred to as "limerance"—the initial intensity of romantic love—is temporary, and usually peters out between eighteen months and three years after your first date, as you settle down to sober reality.

One particularly sneaky aspect of this PEA infatuation is that it effectively camouflages any sexual incompatibility, which doesn't become apparent until the honeymoon phase is over. As Pat Love says, "In the infatuation

Hot Tips: Let's Make a Deal:
The Fine Art of Negotiating Desire

That's right, a deal. The fine art of negotiation. If you and your partner face a desire discrepancy, your chance of improving the situation depends on your ability to communicate and to compromise. While it's certainly easier to blame each other for your mismatched libidos, it's ultimately more productive to work together toward a mutually satisfying solution. This requires a generous amount of give and take, a willingness to look at the big picture, and a recognition that compromise is crucial in any relationship.

- Keep talking. You may be frustrated by your past failures to resolve this issue, but that doesn't mean you can stop talking about it. Restrict your discussions to times when it's equally convenient for both of you to share your thoughts. Do not discuss the situation right after one of you has tried to initiate sex and been turned down by the other—hurt feelings and defensiveness will only muddle your ability to communicate effectively.
- Give yourselves a break. Remember that what you're experiencing is perfectly normal. It's rare for any two people's sexual appetites to be perfectly in synch and unrealistic to expect them to be. Start by giving yourselves permission simply to be yourselves, without apology.
- Practice empathy. Just as you have every right to your sexual feelings, so does your partner. If one of you is feeling guilty and resentful, chances are the other is feeling rejected and unloved. When you're each able to see the situation from the other's viewpoint, you can approach the discussion with more understanding and less finger-pointing.
- Define your terms. It's not enough for one partner to say, "I want more tenderness," or the other to say, "I want more action"—you both need to be specific. You may find that your definitions of "sexual attention" overlap more than you realized.
- Examine your assumptions. The mom who assumes that her partner needs daily sexual attention may be correct, but she might be surprised to learn that she doesn't have to provide it every time. Her husband could be just as happy jerking off to her Victoria's Secret catalog, provided he was assured this wouldn't make her jealous. The husband who'd rather sleep than have sex may have developed a habit of refusing his wife's advances because he

assumes that any sexual encounter has to result in intercourse, which he's not necessarily sure he can get up or stay up for. He might be surprised to learn that his wife would appreciate any kind of sexual expression on his part, and would be perfectly content with letting him set the terms of their encounters.

- Dig deeper. Scratch the surface of your sexual dynamic and you'll uncover the complexities of your larger relationship. Which is to say, whatever problems are affecting your relationship will eventually show up in your bedroom. One of you may need quiet time and tenderness because it provides a break from the demands of childcare, you're depressed about quitting your job, or you can't relax enough to communicate without it. One of you may need nonstop sex because it relieves stress, you crave the ego boost, or it's your preferred way to show affection. By being completely honest with each other you can explore other ways to meet these needs so that your sex life becomes more of a level playing field.

- Share information. Tell your partner what you know or have learned about your sexuality. Let her know that you've discovered your libido fluctuates with your hormones throughout the month, or let him know that a motel room rendezvous far away from that pile of smelly socks on the floor might go a long way to boosting your desire.

- Explore options. Once you've identified problem areas, you can strategize solutions. If you determine that one partner's voracious sexual appetite is a way of fending off stress, discuss other ways of reducing that stress (changing jobs, cutting back hours) or finding other outlets (sports, masturbation, yoga). If you determine that one partner is having a hard time feeling desire, discuss ways of getting in the mood (reading erotica, fantasizing during the day).

- Compromise. Based on the amount of communication you've now done, you may emerge with a new awareness and appreciation of your sexual differences that allows you to accept your sexual dynamic for what it is. Or you may feel the need to change this dynamic, in which case compromises are in order. You might find that a compromise suggests itself when you compare what motivates you to be sexual; most people are motivated by the desire for physical pleasure and intimacy, but crave each to different degrees and achieve each in different ways. Maybe you'd be satisfied by a combination of solo sexual pursuits, periodic sexual encounters with your partner, and more explicit reassurances of your partner's desire for you. Or maybe you'd be satisfied by regular nonsexual massage, periodic sexual encounters with your partner, and a half hour each night for intimate talk or relaxation together. If you practice self-awareness and mutual respect, creative compromise can be surprisingly easy.

- Keep working. As with any plan that involves behavioral change, you will need to evaluate your progress at regular intervals. You'll both always be likely to default to your more polarized positions in times of stress or conflict. Keep the lines of communication open, and don't hesitate to seek professional help if you find the task becomes too big for you to handle alone.

stage, even a low-T person has a significant libido, a significant desire to be sexual. We start to believe that this is the way it always will be, we equate this physical desire with love, and we believe that this infatuation high is true love." During infatuation, it's easy for both of you to assume that your true passionate nature has either finally been uncovered or has finally met its match. If there is a noticeable desire discrepancy between the two of you, it can be particularly disillusioning to bump back down to reality once the limerance phase is over. But don't despair, there are distinct erotic benefits to sticking it out and learning to work with each other's authentic patterns of desire.

Even if you're able to overcome the nostalgia for the good old days of limerance, you may find it hard to overcome nostalgia for the good old days without kids. The reality is that there are now three (or more) of you, and to a certain extent it's irresistible to reminisce longingly about all that loud, spontaneous sex you enjoyed pre-baby. But you can't go home again, mama—at least not until the kids leave home—so you might as well concentrate on creating some equally thrilling memories of the whispered, clandestine sex that's waiting for you to enjoy right here and now.

Attraction

When desire disappears, we sometimes assume that we no longer find our partner attractive. But attraction, like sexual desire, needs to be cultivated. When you first met your partner and were still intoxicated by PEA, all you could register were his or her fine points. Well Cinderella, the spell wears off eventually and then you and your sweetie see each other for who you really are, torn dress, thin hair, and all.

Bearing that in mind, it's possible to stir the embers by remembering what you initially found attractive in your partner. Recalling an early sexual escapade can not only be arousing in itself, but it also helps you identify what it was that turned you on about your beloved—a movement, an attitude, a way of talking, a personality trait, or a particular physical characteristic. Share your memories, and be explicit about what it was that had such an arousing affect on you, and your partner may be inspired to flex his or her charms again. But don't stay stuck in the past. Pay attention to what still gives you visceral pleasure about your partner to this day.

Often our desire fades away because we no longer feel desirable. Biological moms confront a whole host of physical changes, while all moms have to deal with a certain disconnect between the roles of nurturer and hot babe. You may be uncertain about your own attractiveness, and you may project your uncertainty onto a partner. It's important for both of you to discuss your anxieties in as nonconfrontational way as possible.

> I felt really bad about my looks, but was relieved to find out my husband was still very attracted to me. I found that he was being so careful not to make me feel pressured or obligated to have sex that I felt like he wasn't sexually attracted to me. So now we are more open about exactly what is going on.

> My husband has talked about his fear that I'll "let myself go" the way he's seen other moms do and this makes me furious. I have to remind myself that it took him courage to bring it up, but it really feels like an implicit threat that if I become fat and unattractive, he won't love me or want me anymore. I exercise and take care of my body, and I justify it by reminding myself that it's for me, and not about keeping my husband interested.

If your partner suggests that you've been "letting yourself go," it probably did take some courage to make this statement, and it deserves your attention. Of course, the cultural bias that women are expected to prioritize being attractive to men is galling, particularly if you're a biological mom who's expected to snap back into shape overnight. But attraction is a two-way street, and you should feel just as entitled to request that your partner make efforts to keep up his or her appearance for your sake. We're fond of team efforts here—if you plan to diet or join a gym, do it together. If your partner gets the haircut you requested, repay him or her with lavish compliments. If he or she gives you a compliment in return, accept it without making self-deprecating comments. As this biological mom makes abundantly clear, confidence and validation can make all the difference:

> I think that having confidence in your body makes such a wonderful difference with post-baby sex. You just have to think of how hard you worked for those stretch marks, or that extra little lump on your tummy and hips. With positive sexual support from your partner, you can take your sex life and push it back up to where it was before.

Routine

The boredom, the utter boredom, of monogamy.

At the beginning of a love affair, you don't really have much to lose, so it makes sense that you might feel free to take more sexual risks. You can enjoy flexing your seductive powers, experimenting with new sexual activities, or sharing fantasies you once thought you'd never tell another soul. But if the love affair evolves into a committed relationship, the dramatic tension is bound to dissipate, and you soon settle down into a comfortable pattern of familiar routines. Routine inevitably leads to boredom, and boredom leads to a loss of desire.

The trouble is that once you're in a committed relationship, you have a serious emotional investment at stake, which makes it a lot harder to disrupt your routines. You may be afraid you'll hurt your partner's feelings or cause him or her to see you in a less favorable light, so you choose not to rock the boat. The longer you wait to unburden yourself, the harder it becomes. In time, however, you run the risk of getting so bored with your sex life that you no longer desire sex, you resent your partner for not being in tune with your needs, or you assume you're simply no longer attracted to each other. When both partners grow disillusioned with the sex, the resulting "bed death" can be frustrating at best and damaging to the relationship at worst.

If you're not enjoying as much sexual excitement as you'd like—or simply as much sex as you'd like—take the time to question some of your sexual preconceptions. Make a list of the things you'd like to change about your sex life. Be specific! Don't write, "I'd like to be more adventurous," if what you're really fantasizing about is renting a motel room for an hour and tying your girlfriend down to the vibrating bed. Don't write, "I need more romance in my life," if what you're really fantasizing about is listening to your husband read erotic poetry while you soak in a bath filled with rose petals. Then make another list—a list of all the reasons you're unwilling to share these proposals with your partner. You'll probably discover that you have a fair amount of shame about your desires and a lot of assumptions about how he or she will react to them. For example, perhaps you assume that your partner will feel rejected by your desire to introduce a vibrator to your sex play. But maybe deep down you're also afraid that your desire for a "marital aid" indicates that you're somehow defective or abnormal. You may think of yourself as a savvy modern woman, but sexual shame has many disguises, and can creep up when least expected. If you acknowledge the fears you have about your own desires, you'll have a basis for empathy with your partner if he or she is resistant to some of your suggestions.

The prospect of raising the topic of sexual boredom with your partner is bound to make you anxious, but keep in mind that his or her reaction is most likely to be relief. The very fact that you're doing something uncomfortable, that you feel vulnerable, and that you're challenging each other's assumptions can create the erotic tension that may have been missing between you for some time. Either way, you will have taken a crucial first step, because there is absolutely no way to vary your sexual routine unless you talk about it. Communication is the key to ongoing sexual discoveries with a long-term partner, and its rewards are manifold: deepened intimacy, increased sexual self-awareness, and renewed sexual enthusiasm.

I think what I love most about my sex life is that although it is monogamous, I feel a lot of freedom within my relationship to explore sexuality. I feel like the more I'm with my partner, the greater the depth of desire I feel.

Rekindling Passion

Every one of us will take sabbaticals from partner sex at different points throughout our lives. If you're single, you may be on a break right now. If you're in a long-term relationship, you may have already weathered your share of sexual dry spells—or you may be praying for rain this very moment. Parenting presents specific challenges to sustaining your sexual identity, but our suggestions for meeting these challenges will help see you through -all the ups and downs of your erotic life.

We encourage you to make an effort to keep your partnered sex life alive for one simple reason: it's all too easy to lose momentum. While you might think of resuming partner sex after a hiatus as "just like riding a bicycle," it actually feels more like riding a bicycle on a high wire without a net. Fear, awkwardness, and performance anxiety can step in to short-circuit the exchange of erotic energy that used to seem so easy.

> It has now been too long and we are both unsure of where to begin. It seems like once you get out of the habit of regular lovemaking it's hard to get back into it. There is a gap we have to cross to reach one another again, even to think of ourselves as people who have sex. We need to find some kind of continuity.

Physical intimacy isn't necessarily the same as sexual intimacy. Many couples who haven't been sexual for months or years are exceptionally loving and warm with each other. But spooning through the night or holding hands wherever you go doesn't demand the same self-disclosure and risk as an erotic encounter. When you're distracted by your daily obligations and experiencing reduced desire, it's all too easy to lose sight of each other as sexual beings, and it takes an effort to maintain what Jack Morin calls "an erotic playground."[10]

> We are dissatisfied with our sex life. The biggest issue for us to overcome is shyness. We are really careful to work on intimacy in small ways, we talk dirty to one another, and we're trying to make actual genital contact a more regular occurrence in our life.

The good news is that, once you get over the hump, sexual activity can be its own best reward.

> Sometimes I've gone so long without it that I think my body forgets how great it is, and it needs some coaxing. It's like eating when you aren't hungry but know you haven't eaten all day and need it.

Afterwards, I tend to go on a bit of a sex binge, as if I've just discovered sex, and I crave it often.

This is not to suggest that having partner sex after a hiatus automatically results in fireworks. Take advantage of the fact that you won't necessarily be connecting in as effortless or unconscious a way as you once did, and embrace change. This could be a golden opportunity for you and your partner to expand your expectations of a sexual encounter to include a wider range of sensual activities than ever before. If shared pleasure, rather than intercourse or orgasm, is your goal, you'll have a reason to feel desire. And if you cultivate self-awareness in the ways described below, your eroticism will ultimately flourish.

Enjoy yourself

Everything I read about lack of desire just says "oh, it's normal" and doesn't mention what you can possibly DO about it. I miss my sex drive.

If your libido has taken a hike, you don't have to sit and wait for it to come back into view over the horizon. You can get out your sexual compass and track it down. The first step to rediscovering a lost libido is to take the

---

Hot Tips: Rekindling Desire

- Masturbate. Stay connected to your sexuality.
- Fantasize. Give your libido a nudge. Use erotica, adult movies, or make up your own fantasy.
- Touch. Hold hands, embrace, give a sensual shampoo or a massage.
- Kiss. Linger, make eye contact, mean it.
- Remember. Think about what attracted you to your partner, remember a favorite sexual interlude.
- Build Up. Spend the day teasing yourself or your partner sexually.
- Talk. Use email or the phone to express yourself erotically during the day.

focus off the feelings you could or should be having for a partner and pay attention to how your own body feels and what your own imagination is telling you.

Masturbation

You've probably got a running list of all the self-improvements you're convinced would boost your energy and make you a more productive mom—eating well, joining a gym, tucking yourself into bed by 10 PM. Well we want you to add "masturbate" to your list (and we dare you to post it on the fridge). Masturbation is the single best way to stay connected with your sexuality. It allows you to explore your body and mind with ease. Not to mention the fact that it feels good.

> Even though I am currently in a sexual relationship, I never stopped "flying solo" whenever I wanted, which seems to have increased my sex drive, rather than using up my sexual energy.

Whether you're single or partnered, if your libido is ebbing, masturbation provides a low pressure way to boost your sexual self-esteem, cultivate your fantasy life, and enjoy physical release. Masturbation can serve as positive reinforcement for investing time and energy in your own eroticism, and you may discover that a thriving solo sex life boosts your desire for partner sex.

> I think what helped me find my sex drive was starting to masturbate again. They say the more you are sexual the more you want to be sexual, and this has proven true for me. I needed to get back in touch with my sexual side by myself and then begin again with my husband.

Masturbation can also be a helpful tool for couples with desire discrepancies, since it provides an outlet for high desire partners, and a way for low desire partners to recharge their sexual batteries. Furthermore, mutual masturbation can be a highly satisfying alternative to intercourse.

> Sometimes we masturbate together. Sometimes I just watch and vice versa. It's good just to come sometimes. It releases pent up anxiety and frustration.

Fantasies

Sometimes all the libido needs is a little nudge. The reason the brain is called the biggest sex organ is that your imagination plays the biggest role in triggering your arousal. Fantasies can range from fleeting mental images to elaborate mental scenarios. Whether your fantasy is titillating (a flirtatious neighbor) or explicit (a sex fest at the construction site across the street), the bottom line is that it turns you on. If you think you don't fantasize, think again. All of us use our imaginations to enhance our sexual experiences. Pay attention to what thoughts and images pass through your mind while you're masturbating, or when you stand next to an attractive stranger on an elevator. If your fantasy pump needs priming, pick up a book of erotica, rent an X-rated movie, or explore the wealth of explicit materials on-line. Mentally reliving a particularly hot sexual encounter in vivid detail not only makes for great fantasy material, but gives you useful information about what it is that turns you on and why.

Like masturbation, fantasizing can be a nonthreatening way to express your sexual self at times when you don't feel willing or able to be sexual with a partner. And it allows you to keep a sexual spark alive even when you're not partnered.

> I had a little crush on my gay male neighbor. It felt safe and easy. It made me feel sexual again, without having to worry about actually having sex.

> Since my husband left and I haven't had a sexual partner, my erotic dream life has flourished! I've had exquisite sex with a host of friends and famous people, and I inevitably wake up feeling quite satisfied.

Once you have a repertoire of favorite fantasies, you can call on them to help you get in the mood for sex. During your breaks at work or at home, indulge in your fantasies. You may find that weaving a subtle thread of eroticism throughout your day sharpens your sexual appetite.

> It would have been really easy for me to just go and go and never think of sex at all after the birth of the baby. I made it a point to spend at least one day a week thinking of being romantic or sexual with my partner. That way, even if we didn't end up having sex, I didn't get into a rut of forgetting all about it.

Satisfy your senses

Sensual exploration is a bridge that allows you and your partner to reconnect and often to learn something new about each other. If you're trying to rekindle your sex drive, you may find that awakening your senses to their erotic potential is a valuable pick-me-up. If you and your partner are dealing with a desire discrepancy, sensual play can provide you both with pleasurable gratification, while getting you to expand your definition of physical intimacy. Letting go of intercourse or orgasm as the ultimate goal of a sexual encounter has several benefits: it encourages you to experience your entire body as an erogenous zone; it adapts well to a variety of situations; it's conducive to good communication; it relieves performance anxiety; and it can relax as well as energize you.

> We've become a lot more focused on sensation and mutual enjoyment than hardcore sex. Intimacy feels more critical than orgasm right now.

Touch

Many a tired mom looks at sex as just another "chore," but massage is a luxurious indulgence. Hands are capable of communicating much tenderness and affection, so let your fingers do the talking. Massages, foot rubs, back rubs, scalp rubs, and butt rubs can relax a tense mom, who may just discover a new pathway to pleasure along the way:

> Pre-baby we had been doing some power play experimentation, but now we're back to square one and gentle-gentle is what we need. Of course after having our hair pulled and moles picked at all day, a gentle hand is greatly appreciated.
>
> Now I find that massages can lead to intimacy even if we had thought we were too tired. Generally a careful, caring massage can pull me out of even my most exhausted moments.

Similarly, moms should recognize that their partners might be feeling deprived of tactile stimulation. According to Pat Love, despite our cultural stereotype that men value genital sex over cuddling, "Far more men than women, by and large, will tell you that they don't get enough touching, both sexual and non-sexual." Offer to give your partner a bath after she or he gives the baby one!

I try to make sure we spend time together touching each other. It feels good and it makes us feel more connected. I think sleeping together naked helps. I think skin-to-skin bonding is just as important with partners as with kids.

Sight

Between nursing, cuddling, swaddling, and changing, you may be so overloaded that you recoil at the thought of either touching or being touched by your partner. That doesn't mean, however, that you wouldn't appreciate some visual stimulation. This could be a great time to try out a little voyeurism and exhibitionism. You can play the role of adoring fan while your partner strips, masturbates, or works out in the buff. Try looking at an erotic art book or a racy film together. Whether you decide to get physical, or you're content just to watch, you get to enjoy a potent new source of arousal.

Sound

Do you know what kind of music turns your partner on? If so, make a tape of his or her favorite erotic tunes and spend a candlelit evening dancing or kissing to the music. If you don't know, it's time you found out! You could make a game out of it one night: "Name the sexiest song from your teen years?" or "What artist best captures sex in his/her music?" etc. Use your new-found knowledge to set the scene for a later encounter.

Also, try to expand how you verbally express affection. Go beyond the generic "I love you," and get specific: describe which of his or her traits particularly appeal to you, or reminisce about the first time you met. Whispering dirty secrets may incite your partner's lust; if you need practice, pick up a copy of *Talk Sexy to the One You Love* or *Exhibitionism for the Shy*.

Smell

Ever noticed your partner getting a little randy while baking pumpkin pie? Have your eyes ever glazed over at the smell of black licorice? Did you know that the aroma of these two ingredients, combined with cucumber, baby powder, and lavender, can increase female sexual arousal? That, at least, is according to the hard-working researchers at the Smell and Taste Treatment and Research Foundation in Chicago (and you thought ice-cream tasters had the best jobs).[11]

For decades scientists, chemists, and perfume manufacturers have been trying to identify and synthesize pheromones—odorless molecules emitted by animals and humans, which supposedly are detected by an organ in our nose and trigger sexual attraction. The degree to which researchers have been able to recreate these chemical secretions is debatable (studies have found that men's cologne actually decreases women's arousal), but there's no denying that the nose plays a role in sexual arousal.

Sadly, our sense of smell tends to get assaulted more than appreciated these days. But if an aversion to heavy perfumes, pollution, car exhaust, or baby poop can do anything for you, it can serve to remind you to seek out pleasurable alternatives. Make a point of discovering what scents please your partner, and incorporate these into your routine. If he loves the smell of fresh air after a rain, go for a walk after a storm. If she loves gardenias, put some by her bed, or put scented oil into her bath. By reintegrating these subtle but profound pleasure-triggers into your lives, you can experience sensuality as an everyday delight.

Taste

We ourselves are so fond of food that it's no stretch for us to equate the euphoria that accompanies eating a delicious meal with the euphoria that accompanies sex. In both cases, we enjoy exquisite anticipation, a consummation that stimulates all the senses, and pleasurable satiation. There's a reason lavish feasts have often been depicted as sexual foreplay. Unfortunately, with small kids around, meal time feels more like a three-ring circus than a Roman orgy or the lobster scene from *Tom Jones*. Take our advice: leave the macaroni and cheese to the kids and set your set your sights higher. Call the baby-sitter and treat yourself to a night out. Put the kids to bed early and order up your favorite take-out (with Web access, options abound for urban moms). If you can't afford to go out, take turns preparing a gourmet meal for each other. If you don't already know what foods tantalize your lover's taste buds, find out and get cooking! If you tend to do most of the cooking you may find that having someone else cook for you is just as pleasurable as eating the meal.

As for foods which are reputed to be infused with aphrodisiac powers, we're here to tell you not to break the bank seeking out rhino horn and oysters. While there's no scientific proof that certain delicacies are sexual stimulants, there's certainly something to be said for the placebo effect, so if you've convinced yourself that crème caramel is the culinary Viagra, feast away.

Make your mood

Sexual excitement is often made, not born. Sure, desire can wash over you when you least expect it, but more often you have to take some initiative to get yourself in the mood. This can be as simple as enjoying a fantasy daydream on the way to work, or as elaborate as planning a romantic weekend out of town. In the past, you may not always have been aware of the ways in which you were priming yourself to experience desire. Now that you're a mom, you're going to have to put some serious energy into creating the mood, or desire will get so tangled up in that pile of sippy-cups, birthday party invitations, and dirty laundry that it will never penetrate your consciousness. But don't worry—cultivating desire is fun (much more fun than washing sippy-cups, mailing party invitations, or sorting laundry). All that's required is self-awareness, respect for your own feelings, receptivity to your partner's feelings, and the occasional leap of faith.

You've got to be self-aware in order to be realistic about when and under what conditions you'd be interested in sex. For example, these women realize that there's no chance they'll feel desire unless they can achieve some distance from their children:

> When my stepdaughter arrived to stay with us for a while I was so nervous that we would wake her that I found it difficult to relax and enjoy myself.

> Unless I feel secure that the kids are 100% asleep, out of the house being watched by someone else, or otherwise not in my "mom radar," I cannot focus entirely on physical pleasure.

You've got to respect your own feelings so you won't be pressured into a sexual encounter that doesn't meet your needs. This might mean that you have to take primary responsibility for initiating sex.

> I find that since the birth of the children, my husband is much less likely to initiate sex. When we discussed it, he said this was because he knows how hard it is for me to be home with three children all day long, so if I've had a long day, he doesn't want to push me into sex that I might not be up for. So I initiate sex much more often than he does, but it's okay with both of us.

But you also need to be receptive to your partner's feelings or both of you run the risk of getting bogged down in the dreaded initiation wars. The worst-case scenario is that you get stuck in a classic initiation stand-off, with one of you assuming the role of "insensitive horndog" and the other assuming the role of "frigid wet blanket." Some couples can get so polarized that they have a hard time experiencing any physical contact without diving for their respective bunkers.

> When the baby goes to sleep, I just want to be alone, but my husband sees this as an opportunity to have sex. It's hard because sometimes he's just being sweet and affectionate, but I assume he always wants it to end in sex, so I get cold and unresponsive.

The key to breaking this self-defeating cycle is to meet each other halfway. Put the emphasis on identifying what you want out of sex and when you want it. As Pat Love suggests, "When you say no, say when. When you say no, say what. What really hurts relationships is a flat out rejection or refusal." In other words, instead of snapping, "Quit poking at me," you could say, "I really just want to go to sleep in your arms right now, but Saturday morning when the kids are watching cartoons, you're all mine."

You may be thinking, but what if I don't want to be poked at now or on Saturday morning? That's where the leap of faith comes in. To a certain extent where sexual desire is concerned, you need only be willing and optimistic. You may be initially ambivalent about a sexual encounter, but if you allow yourself to be receptive to your partner's advances, you invite the possibility that a flicker of interest can be fanned into a flame of desire:

> I have found that no matter how tired or overworked or underappreciated I may feel at times, that I must remind myself that this person who wants to have sex with me is the love of my life, my partner, my daughter's father, and my best friend. I sometimes have to remind myself how much I really enjoy sex, how I have always liked a good fuck.

Although we appreciate the spirit behind the "just do it" approach to partner sex, this attitude only works if you feel that you have the leeway to negotiate your terms or to back out of an encounter if desire simply doesn't develop. Having sex out of obligation or fear is just about the most negative reinforcement around:

> I would have sex when I didn't want to and that would make me feel like never having sex again.

The bottom line is that you need to take responsibility for requesting what would or wouldn't give you genuine pleasure. Sex should never be a service you provide for a partner or one more task to cross off your to-do list. Sure, sometimes you'll be compromising with a partner, but by definition a compromise means there's something in it for you! Once you learn what stimulates your desires, you can make your own mood, instead of passively waiting to fall into it.

> I think of sex as a way of pampering myself. I take advantage of any impromptu blocks of time when my children are out of the picture. My partner is usually ready to go anytime, so I tend to initiate the unexpected sessions. If it's been a while, sometimes we rent a porno to really rev things up. I'm definitely of a lower libido, but am happy that our sex life has gotten to a middle frequency that satisfies us both. This has taken a good three years.

Success Is Its Own Reward

Sexual desire can seem like a magician's rabbit—one minute it disappears into thin air, the next it reemerges with the flourish of a top hat. But you have the ability to master a trick or two yourself; all it takes is a little strategically applied compassion, humor, reflection, and perseverance. We're encouraging you to devote respect and attention to cultivating your sexual desires, not only because you deserve a rich and rewarding sex life, but because your kids deserve you to have one. Your children are watching you to determine what it means to be an adult, and if all they see is your daily grind of working and care taking, they'll never want to grow up and leave home (and you'll never get to explore the erotic possibilities of the empty nest!). Whether you're single and dating, or coparenting with a spouse, take advantage of every opportunity to enjoy—and let your kids witness—the pleasures of adult relationships.

Hot Tips: Tips from Other Moms

Just Go for It
I find that with sex, the more I have it, the sexier I feel, and therefore the more comfortable I am with going after it, getting what I want during it, and giving my husband what he wants.

Let Your Anxieties Go
I feel really good about myself sexually during lovemaking. For that length of time I forget that I weigh more than I'd like or that I have responsibilities to the babies. It's like a trip back to my "me" self.

Stay Physical
I have to have physical contact with my partner at least once a week, even if it's only for an hour during nap time. Intercourse isn't the point. We just need an intimacy that reminds us that we're people independent of the little one.

Get Adult Time
Sex allows me to feel like an adult and a woman, which is important after spending a day conversing with a three-year-old.

Get Perspective
We understand that sex has different roles in our lives. It can be fun, it can be romantic, it can just help deal with stress. It helps for getting a good night sleep. It can take hours or minutes. I think the best is that we respect and trust each other. Sex is not used to prove anything, it's just a great way to show our love and affection.

Make a sex date
That way I can be mentally and physically prepared and we can work best together to get the kids in bed. It also helps me if I get some positive nonsexual touching in the form of massage before we have sex. That way I approach it feeling more relaxed and comfortable with my body.

Help your partner find other outlets
He wanted sex all the time when I didn't, but he got over it. He learned to channel his energies into creative projects and self-pleasuring, researching ways to improve his love-making skills, etc.

Be spontaneous
Go for it. We used to tease a lot about who wanted to have sex, who was the initiator—now we don't. You can get a lot done in twenty minutes. I think that it's important to remain affectionate with both the baby and your partner.

You know what having a child has taught us that I think is most important? To try to treat each other as well as we treat him. We realized that we'd fuck everything up if we treated him well but treated each other terribly. He won't learn how to expect a relationship, or how to make a relationship good, if he doesn't see it around him.

8

Reinventing Sex
as a Parent

Many of us, regardless of our chronological age, don't think of ourselves as being truly grown-up until we become parents. You're probably well aware that parenting has enhanced your emotional maturity, but you may not have thought much about the ways in which it can enhance your sexual maturity. After all, our culture perpetuates a model of arrested development with regard to sexual expression, and we get precious little encouragement to evolve past the stage of cootie-alerts and adolescent peer pressure to a self-assured adult eroticism. But in fact, if you want your sex life not only to survive but to thrive post-parenthood, you're going to have to grow up about sex. The good news is that becoming a sexual grown-up is fun: you get to take responsibility for your own pleasure, show some initiative, develop your creativity, and be as "wanton" as you wanna be.

You Get to Take Responsibility

Women are susceptible to a certain passivity when it comes to sex. We're socialized to put our sexual energies into being appealing and enticing, into being the fetching flowers that draw the attention of swarms of buzzing suitors. All too often, our eroticism is defined by our efforts to inspire desire in someone else: "What do I want? I want him/her to want me!" It's perfectly valid to enjoy the ego gratification of being a seductive siren, but if this is your default mode of sexual expression, you are missing out on a world of uncensored pleasure. It's human to want to be a desirable sex object, but it's divine to be a sexual subject. By "sexual subject," we mean someone who feels pure lust for her partner, who wants to get her hands on her lover's body and express her desire so actively that any concerns about whether she herself is good-enough, pretty-enough, or has-her-gut-sucked-in-far-enough fly right out the window.

> After my son was born, I felt very unsexy for about a year, but then I had an affair with a woman and I felt free as a bird and could care less. I still sometimes feel fat and very unsexy when I'm trying on clothes at stores, but then I read *Hip Mama* or call up my girlfriend and I feel sexy all over again.

Sexual subjectivity is a declaration of independence—independence from passivity, insecurity, and self-censorship. Once you cease defining your sexuality in reactive terms, you're no longer solely dependent on your lovers for ego or sexual gratification.

> I enjoy sex more often than my husband, so a vibrator has helped me not feel neglected. I realize my husband can not please me every night, so my new vibrator has become a great friend.

Becoming a mother can be a valuable catalyst for transforming your erotic approach from reactive to proactive. In an adult relationship, love is inevitably colored by anxiety about reciprocation: which one of us loves the other more? It's empowering to discover your own capacity to love your children unconditionally, to enjoy feelings that aren't contingent on the responses they elicit. Parenting is positive reinforcement to break out of the reactive mode of relating; once you do you're less likely to base your self-worth on other people's opinions of you. The ability to identify and value your personal experience is fundamental to a satisfying sexuality.

> The big issue was, hey, I'm getting older, isn't it about time we had a fabulous sex life? Having children made me realize I've got to get on with living my life—it's going by so fast! I can't settle for so-so sex anymore, so I let it be known if I'm not enjoying myself, and I no longer have "mercy" sex. When one of us wants sex, the other doesn't "just oblige."

> We told each other what we really like in bed, not just ooh-aah, baby, but stuff that was almost embarrassing and very hard to reveal. We did it a little at a time and kinda played it out as we went along. Now sex is amazing.

Motherhood often brings a healthy pragmatism into the bedroom. For one thing, when your time and energy are limited, you're motivated to cut to the chase and assert what you want when you want it. And the realities of parenting can be a good antidote to a variety of romantic illusions. Women who discover how difficult it is to figure out what a crying baby wants, who struggle to soothe an upset toddler, or who come to realize that so-called maternal instinct boils down to repeated trial and error are less likely to get hung up on old saws like "If you loved me, you'd know how to please me without my saying a word."

> I feel that my gratification is my priority, because I don't have time to mess around and not be fully satisfied! I think my partner and I are both more communicative now, about what we want, when we want it, and when we need to go to sleep. We were both a little shy on these things BB (before baby).

> We've learned that we both have needs and that neither one of us can read minds. We need to let our needs be known, in a nice way of course. If we don't know what to do, we can't do it.

The silver (latex) lining: safer sex

Must we really point out that you can't take responsibility for your sexuality without taking responsibility for your sexual health? Do you really need one more reminder of the myriad reasons to practice safer sex? Alas, perhaps we must and perhaps you do—certainly plenty of sexually active adults have their heads permanently stuck in the sand when it comes to the topic of sexually transmissible diseases (STDs). Yet the fact of the matter is that sexual contact—specifically the contact between pre-come, semen, vaginal secretions, blood, and the mucous membranes of mouth, vagina, and anus—is a highly efficient way of transmitting viruses and bacteria from one person to another. This doesn't mean that sex is inherently dirty and dangerous, any more than your toddler's repeated bouts with head lice and the flu mean that a childcare center is inherently dirty and dangerous. It just means that any sexual grown-up owes it to herself to get a handle on some basic hygiene and to get her hands on some condoms, water-based lube, and gloves. The good news about safer sex is that following these simple precautions displays respect for you and your partners, inspires peace of mind, and enhances the creativity of your sex play.

Hot Tips: Safer Sex 101

- Use condoms for vaginal or anal intercourse.
- Consider using condoms for oral sex (they can be cut open for cunnilingus or oral/anal sex, or you can use saran wrap); while unprotected oral sex hasn't been definitively linked to HIV transmission, herpes, hepatitis B, and bacterial infections can all be transmitted orally.
- Use condoms on shared sex toys or when you're moving a toy from anus to vagina.
- Use only water-based lubes with latex condoms or gloves; any oil or petroleum-based product will destroy latex.
- If you have latex allergies, use polyurethane condoms and gloves; polyurethane isn't as stretchy and supple as latex, but it is stronger and thinner.
- Don't use lambskin condoms; they are permeable to viruses.

If you're single and dating, practicing safer sex should be a given. Even if you're comfortable both asking and telling about your sexual histories, neither you nor your date can guarantee having all the facts about all your past partners. If you're in a monogamous relationship, and you and your partner have tested negative for HIV, hepatitis B, hepatitis C, syphilis, gonorrhea, chlamydia, and you've never had an outbreak of genital warts or herpes, you may feel comfortable foregoing safer sex precautions. But if you haven't been screened for all of the above, you should be—certain STDs are symptomless, and can cause serious health problems if left undetected: for instance, chlamydia can result in Pelvic Inflammatory Disease and genital warts are the leading cause of cervical cancer. Given the six-month window period for HIV infection (it can take up until six months after infection before our bodies produce the antibodies that would be detected in an HIV test), you would need to practice safer sex for six months after the first HIV test and then repeat the test in order to confirm a negative result.

Unlike bacterial infections, viral infections can't be treated with a simple course of antibiotics, and you and your partners will have to deal with these on an ongoing basis. Therefore, if you're positive for a viral STD—such as herpes, HIV, or hepatitis B—you'll need to develop your safer sex repertoire in order to enjoy the sex life you deserve. Too often, information about safer sex is presented in terms of preventing "the clean folks" from crossing over and becoming "the diseased." Anyone who's ever had an STD knows how painful and damaging this attitude can be. Furthermore, it's nonsense—the whole point of safer sex techniques is that they allow sexual activity for one and all.

Whether you're with a long-term partner or a hot new date, whether you're STD-positive or STD-negative, safer sex is an erotic playground well worth exploring. Condoms are available in a wide range of colors, sizes, shapes, textures, and flavors. Gloves cover dry skin and rough cuticles, transforming hands into smooth, slippery organs of pleasure. Many men report that condoms help prolong their erection, and that applying lubricant to both the inside and the outside of the condom enhances sensation. You may feel more willing to explore the pleasures of anal eroticism—from rimming to fingering to penetration—with a barrier in place. Safer sex supplies encourage communication, introduce humor, and expand creative possibilities. Plus, if your partners are men, condoms are highly effective contraceptives.

Basically, it's up to you to learn the facts, consider your options, and create your own risk management plan. This may mean that you follow different safer sex guidelines for different encounters. Practicing safer sex is a way of taking responsibility, showing initiative, and prioritizing your sex life—just the ticket for sexual adults like you.

You Get to Make Time

Many parents can testify that the key to maintaining an active sex life is planning. As discussed in the Having It All chapter, kids generate more than their fair share of distractions, and if you don't make an effort, it's just too darn easy to "forget" to have sex.

Weeks may go by and we don't connect sexually. This is often misunderstood as "where have you gone? don't you want me?" but the truth is, we just get caught up with the kids and all that they involve.

You might initially find that one of the biggest challenges to maintaining an active sex life is letting go of the idea that sex should be spontaneous. The cult of spontaneity—the belief that unplanned sexual encounters are somehow more authentic or pleasurable than premeditated encounters—has quite a hold on our collective erotic imagination. For decades, popular movies, novels, and love songs have promoted the romantic notion that sex entails being swept off our feet and overwhelmed by passion. There's some pretty obvious sexual shame lurking beneath all that bodice-ripping—we're reluctant to put any forethought into having sex, because we're reluctant to acknowledge that we want to have sex! Sexual desire is supposed to sneak up on us and override our inhibitions.

Of course, you wouldn't have much patience with a teenager telling you, "Oops, I didn't know I was going to have sex until it just happened!" Surely you can marshal at least as much responsibility and self-awareness as you'd want your kids to exhibit. And the truth is you probably don't feel sandbagged by desire all that often. Couples who have been in long-term relationships soon learn that they need to be proactive in strategizing ways to stay sexually motivated, and this goes doubly for parents. As it turns out, their are myriad benefits to planning sexual encounters. Haven't you ever noticed that the planning stage is one of the most exciting aspects of a trip? Looking forward to a premeditated encounter is not only a powerful aphrodisiac, but enjoyably arousing in and of itself.

Planning sex allows you to create the mood that best sparks your desire, to shift gears from mom mode to lover mode, and to guarantee you'll be prepared with birth control, safer sex accouterments, lubricant, or sex toys. Best of all, if you schedule a shopping spree at the thrift store, you can enjoy the best of both worlds by staging that bodice-ripping scene in your very own bedroom.

I visit the Salvation Army regularly to buy my daughter dress-up clothes, and I've discovered that costumes are fun for grown-ups too! When she was off on a sleepover last Saturday, I lounged around the house in a strapless evening dress and feather boa—quite inspiring to my boyfriend.

You may be resistant to the idea of planned sex due to performance anxiety—it's common to assume that planned encounters will feel uncomfortably awkward and staged. In fact, the prospect of sex in which both partners are fully awake and fully present can be a little unnerving. Feeling a little off-balance won't ruin your mood, but the expectation that sex should be a silent, efficiently scripted event just might.

Hot Tips: Tips from Other Moms

Take advantage of work time.
My partner and I often take a few minutes to call each other and talk about what we plan to do to each other later, or just say I love you. No kids around and it makes us both feel loved and appreciated.

Communicate every day.
We talk or phone or leave notes or email each other every day to discuss how to cope with the child, or how hot we are for each other.

Send suggestive emails.
With a toddler sharing our bed, it's hard. We do a lot more sexy emails, suggestive phone messages, etc. We talk about sex a lot, only manage it a few times a month. There is a bit more self-satisfying going on.

Go for quality over quantity.
Since the quantity is so much less, the quality has to be better. It's more special when you do find the time. You're more adventurous and creative in your lovemaking. It has made me more inhibitionless and daring in my sex.

Send sexy nonverbal cues.
We exchange glances, subtle touches, when no one is looking. We can play all day with each other, and then when we finally have a chance to get to the bedroom it is like having had hours and hours of foreplay. Even when we just play, the satisfaction of sharing an intimate glance with my husband is wonderful.

There's such a gap between the media portrayal of sex and sex as it really is: we don't have orgasms every time, it can be clumsy, there are good times and bad times. Some people's expectations of sex just don't seem real.

You'll be much more likely to enjoy the time you and your partner have set aside to be together if you approach it with an "anything goes" spirit of playfulness. Maybe you'll swap some erotic massage; maybe you'll describe your current favorite fantasy while you both masturbate side-by-side; maybe you'll put on an X-rated video with the sound muted and invent your own dialogue. You get to decide together what you'd like to do, or what not to do. The beauty of regularly scheduled sexual encounters is that there will always be a next time to try something else.

We eventually worked out a standing playdate for our kidlet on Sunday afternoons. Every two weeks he goes to his little friend's house, and we have three glorious hours to tear a piece off each other—whatever we want. This time is sacred, and is never to be squandered on repainting the dining room. We fill in the holes with night and morning sex, but he is not a night boy and I am NOT a morning girl, so those Sundays are the cement that holds us together sexually.

You Get to Have Fun

You've no doubt watched the expression on a child's face as she jumps in a mud puddle or he comes barreling down a playground slide—it is one of sheer delight. Our own children teach us a valuable lesson to apply to sex: playfulness. Somewhere along the path to adulthood we trade in bruised knees for bruised egos, an appetite for adventure for a comfortable routine, and unbridled enthusiasm for sensible restraint. When it comes to sex, we take ourselves far too seriously, inhibiting ourselves out of fear that we'll do or say something wrong, we'll fail our partner, we'll get messy, or we'll embarrass ourselves. But it's precisely the risk-taking, the adventure, and the down-and-dirtiness that keep sex from getting boring. Without that spark, sex starts to feel like a chore, and our desire diminishes significantly. In other words, being a satisfied sexual adult just might involve behaving more like a kid.

A toy chest of your own

Did you know that sex toys have a long and illustrious history? Dildos, for example, have been found among Paleolithic stone sculptures dating back over thirty thousand years. Leather and wooden dildos feature prominently in ancient Greek religious rituals, comedies, and vase paintings, and there are references to dildos in the Kama Sutra and Asian pillow books. More recently, electric vibrators were invented by American doctors in the late nineteenth century as an aid in the treatment of women's "hysteria." As historian Rachel Maines reveals, medical experts of the day believed that women suffered from a variety of physical and nervous disorders that could be soothed via genital massage and orgasm—since vibrations were applied to the clitoris, not inside the vagina, "pelvic massage" was considered a perfectly respectable clinical remedy. Vibrators quickly became popular consumer appliances, marketed directly to the public in "ladies" magazines and the Sears Roebucks catalog, where they were promoted as palliatives for a whole host of ailments from asthma to tuberculosis. In fact, vibrators were the fifth home appliance to be electrified (following the sewing machine, fan, teakettle, and toaster, but preceding the vacuum cleaner or steam iron).[1] Once vibrators began appearing in the stag films of the twenties, their respectability became considerably tarnished and they dropped off the pages of needlepoint magazines!

While dildos no longer have ritual significance, and vibrators are no longer medically prescribed, sex toys continue to delight playful adults to this day. A 1997 survey found that 10% of sexually active adults use sex toys in partner sex,[2] which means that literally millions of women and men around the country are slipping between the sheets with erotic accessories. But that doesn't mean they're talking about it—even those of us who are comfortable browsing the adult shelves of our local video and book stores aren't likely to swap vibrator recommendations with our pals. After all, the topic of sex toys inevitably inspires snickers and jokes about trips to the emergency room. It's hard to shake popular stereotypes of sex toys as unnatural devices used by folks who are compensating for their own deficiencies: they're often viewed as either "marital aids" designed to "fix" a sexual problem, devices to console the lonely, or accouterments for the kinky.

The truth is that an adult's desire to bring sex toys into bed isn't any more kinky than a child's desire to bring bath toys into the tub. Toys offer expanded sensation and stimulate imaginative play. A silk scarf, an ostrich feather, and a clitoral vibrator all afford tactile stimulation. A partner's fingers, penis, and a dildo all provide pleasurable pressure and fullness. When you wrap a cock ring around his penis, or slip a blindfold over her eyes, you get to explore the erotic territory where mind and body converge. Despite a common fear that toys (especially vibrators) will get you "addicted" to a specific form of stimulation, they're much more likely to help you break out of a rut in your sex life. If anything, experimenting with toys can expand your awareness of the myriad erotic possibilities of the world around you, suffusing your visits to the hardware store or the produce stand with a new sense of pleasurable purpose. After over a decade of selling vibrators, we ourselves remain unabashed boosters of the joys of toys and refer you to the Resources section for some reliable sources.

> As a new mom, I discovered that sex toys helped me adjust to my changed body. It's a positive spin on thinking of your body in a new way—new toys create new and different responses.

Enjoying erotica

Since becoming a parent, you've surely honed your skills at reading aloud. Why limit your bedtime reading to Dr. Seuss and Madeline? Recent years have seen an explosion in erotica and sexual self-help books. You can read to your lover from erotic anthologies encompassing a stunning range of styles and subject matters, or study up on every conceivable sexual wrinkle, including how to get in touch with your inner dominatrix, stimulate your chakras through Tantric breathing techniques, enjoy your girlfriend's G-spot, talk dirty, massage your boyfriend's prostate with a strap-on dildo, or give better head. The Web is also an outstanding resource both for sex information and erotica.

> My husband and I both surf the Internet and send each other links from sites that have "how to" ideas.

Adult videos offer their own special blend of home entertainment and sexual inspiration. While you may feel like this survey respondent who's frustrated by the low production values of many mainstream porn films, plenty of women and couples are flocking to video rental stores and have learned to identify specific directors, producers, or performers who reliably float their boats.

> Would you please donate a portion of your income from this book
> to an arts endowment fund created for improving the quality of
> erotic films?

It does help to have realistic expectations when you rent or purchase an erotic video. Sure, production values are low, the soundtrack may be hokey, and plots, acting, and script are usually minimal. That's because most adult videos are made on a low budget; they aren't designed to inspire your aesthetic sensibilities, they're designed to inspire sexual arousal. If you can let go of your judgments and zero in on your visceral responses, you'll probably find that viewing porn is an entertaining way to create a mood, stimulate your imagination, expand your fantasies, or give you new tricks to try at home. Check our Resources section for recommendations of retail and mail order companies that offer more discriminating selections of both erotic and educational sex videos. And if you don't like the erotica you find, make some of your own!

> Writing erotic poetry and photographing myself have helped me in
> my sexual discovery and given me an outlet for my sexual energy.

A word about lube

> My sex life was saved by fantasies, humor, and lubricant in a tube.

Allow us to propose a toast to one of the most humble, yet most versatile, erotic accessories ever invented: water-based lubricant. Lube is the simple ingredient that can help transform a humdrum sexual encounter into the slippery, messy, glorious affair it deserves to be. Genital tissue is sensitive, and rewards tender, loving care. Without moisture, the friction of genital stimulation can be distinctly counter-erotic. With moisture, penetration is more pleasurable, clitoral stimulation is more enticing, and gliding against your partner's body feels downright luxurious.

Both women and men often subscribe to the false notion that women "should" provide sufficient vaginal lubrication to handle any erotic occasion, and that a loss of natural lube reflects a lack of arousal. The truth is that a vast array of hormonal and environmental factors affect vaginal lubrication. The hormonal shifts of your menstrual cycle, and decreased estrogen—either postpartum, while breastfeeding, after a hysterectomy, or after menopause—

can all reduce lubrication. Reduced estrogen levels also result in the thinning of vaginal tissues, which is one more reason to pour on the lube. Stress, allergy medications, alcohol, smoking, and jet lag are among the many environmental factors that can dry up your mucous membranes.

Essentially, there's no excuse not to use lube! It's a valuable safer sex accessory, since well-lubricated latex creates less friction, is less likely to tear, and feels vastly more pleasurable for both parties. Lubricant allows you to enjoy much longer sessions of lovemaking, and it's crucial to use for any anal penetration (since the tissues of the rectum produce no natural lubrication and are much more delicate than the tissues of the vagina). Water-based lubricants are now available in a truly staggering array of formulas, ranging from thick and gel-like, to smooth and silky, so there is bound to be one out there that has your name on it.

Fantasies and role-playing

Kids everywhere relish role-playing, dress-up, fantasy adventures, and story-telling, and all these elements of play are valuable mood-enhancers for amorous adults. Let your own imagination run wild, and you may find that play-acting is just what's needed to refresh your erotic perspective. Whether you're dressing up as "cowboy and schoolmarm," or simply rejecting the societal roles that don't conform to your own erotic reality, the sense of unlimited possibilities can be hugely liberating—and arousing.

> Don't think you have to have parent sex, whatever that is. Sometimes people think they have to have nice, mellow sex after children, when what they really need is the back-against-the-wall, foot-on-the-windowsill kind.

Most folks have fantasies that fall into two categories: "the impossible dream" or "the unforgettable reality." In other words, you can be aroused by fantasies of adventures that you would never, or could never, enjoy in real life (seducing your favorite movie star, having weightless sex in a spaceship). And you can be aroused by reality-based fantasies, those that draw on memories of past encounters or visions of future encounters. You probably enjoy your own "impossible dream" fantasies without too much shame or anxiety, and you're probably comfortable with your partner's. However, you may be a little more ashamed or threatened by each other's reality-based fantasies. One of the challenges—and rewards—of becoming a sexual grown-up is learning to accept and enjoy the richness of the erotic imagination. In order to do so, you need to overcome the following common inhibitors.

Feeling left out

You'd doubtless be pleased and flattered to learn that your sweetie boosts his or her arousal during sex by reminiscing about particularly hot encounters you've shared in the past. But if it turns out that some of his or her most powerful fantasies revolve around other past lovers, or the cute babe who just moved in next door, you might feel a little threatened. Given our scarcity issues around erotic expression, we often fall into the trap of viewing lust as an either/or proposition— "If my husband desires her, he doesn't really desire me," or "If my girlfriend is turned on by attributes I don't have, she's not turned on by me anymore."

> My husband fantasizes about younger women who are not mothers and that hurts me a lot.

The truth is we're all capable of being aroused by many different people and many different attributes. Enjoying a fantasy about a past lover one day, and a fantasy about a current lover the next is a natural way of keeping your erotic appetite stimulated. If you're so inclined, and feel secure enough to explore each other's fantasies with an open mind, you might notice that certain recurring themes are more responsible for your arousal than the actual cast of characters. And these themes—for instance, anticipation, teasing, virgin experiences, emotional closeness, being overpowered—can give you valuable information as to how to turn up the heat in your sex life (see Jack Morin's *The Erotic Mind* for more on this subject).

Feeling abnormal

Many people are comfortable with fantasies that they identify as "politically incorrect"—such as those that involve dominance and submission, exhibitionism, voyeurism, or inappropriate partners—because they're confident that they don't plan to enact them. After all, fantasies around taboo behavior are understandably common, since forbidden fruit has a powerful erotic charge. A certain amount of shame or ambivalence about your fantasies can have the positive effect of making them more potent and pleasurable. However, if you would like to incorporate elements from your fantasies into your sexual reality, this ambivalence becomes problematic. People who share their fantasies with a partner are especially vulnerable to anxieties about whether their own or their partner's fantasies are "normal."

In fact, whether your fantasies are normal is not the point. The point is to determine what aspects from your fantasy life you and your partner might like to explore together. All too often, when couples raise the topic of expanding their sexual repertoire, their shame and embarrassment polarizes them. The shame can be: "Gosh, I must be a pervert if I want to be tied to the bed during oral sex," or the shame can be: "Gosh, I must be a prude if I don't want to tie her to the bed during oral sex." We easily default to a sense of insecurity and deficiency both around the sexual desires we have and those we lack. This can lead to a cycle in which each blames the other for being either too demanding or too much of a wet blanket, very negative reinforcement for further confidences. As the survey respondent quoted below suggests, a sense of trust and acceptance are often prerequisites to sexual adventurousness.

> I'm open to things now that I would have recoiled in horror at ten years ago. It's nice to be really settled with the same partner for a decade and to have worked through untold amounts of relationship junk so we can really be friends and not worry about: "Is he happy with me? Is he going to find someone else better?" Knowing that this is it, that yes we are committed and in love, enables me to be open to his suggestions of things that I'm not totally comfortable with at first, often to discover that they're great. In the end, Settling Down has created the balance we need for very relaxed and intense sex.

It's perfectly all right if one of you fantasizes about activities that the other doesn't wish to try. The whole point of being entitled to your desires is that neither of you is more or less entitled than the other.

> Since experiencing a return of my libido, I would like to try swinging, but my husband does not. But he is willing to try almost anything I want to in the bedroom. I desired anal sex, and since we started playing with that, I have discovered a whole new realm of pleasure. I would love to try a double penetration with two men, but doubt he would agree to it. Even so, we communicate more about sex now than we ever have, kids or no kids.

Fantasy is a powerful tool for self-awareness, and we encourage you to embrace, explore, and elaborate on your own wherever they may lead you. Whether they manifest as random thoughts, mental images, or scenarios you role-play with a partner, it is your fantasies that transform tactile stimulation into full-blown erotic arousal. They deserve your curiosity, respect, and appreciation.

Hot Tips: Give the Gift of Pleasure

You don't have to wait around for "the mood" to strike, you can make it happen with a bit of advance planning. These are the types of gifts that are as much fun to give as they are to receive.

- Give your partner a child-free day. Leave it open-ended so the recipient can claim the gift when he or she most needs it. This nonsexual gift allows your partner the valuable privacy and opportunity to relax and refuel that could be all he or she needs to feel renewed enthusiasm for sexual intimacy.
- Plan a romantic evening and give your partner a hand-written invitation. Arrange everything yourself—the baby-sitting, the dinner, the ambiance—don't let him or her lift a finger. You can do this at your own house or you can combine it with a night at a bed and breakfast.
- Give your partner an erotic bath. Pull out all the stops—set the mood with candles, scented oils, and heated towels. Throw in a slow, luxurious hand and foot massage.
- Give your partner a coupon good for a trip to a sex toy store where he or she can pick out any item desired. Or buy a gift certificate and tuck it inside a toy catalog.
- Plan an erotic video viewing night. You can do this after the kids are asleep if you're not too tired. Rent several. Let your partner have complete control of the remote!
- Write your partner a sexy letter. You can retell the story of how you met, describe his or her most attractive features, relive one of your favorite sexual encounters, or detail what naughty things you'd like to do in the future.

You Get to Redefine Sex

If you've been a parent for more than a month or two, you've probably figured that when it comes to raising children: a) everybody's an expert; and b) nobody's expertise except your own is worth squat. You can devour parenting books for tips and guidelines, but ultimately, you're the one who knows the individual quirks and personalities of your family members best, and you're in the best position to decide how to interact with your child. As Sheila Kitzinger puts it:

> It is not just a matter of a mother performing an action, such as breast-feeding a baby, but of how she feels about what she does— and whether or not she behaves in an easy, spontaneous, and above all self-assured way may be a good deal more important than the system of child-rearing she adopts.[3]

By now, you can tell where we're going with this. Yes, you can devour sex books for tips and guidelines, but ultimately, you're the one who knows the individual quirks of your eroticism. Your self-assurance about the kind of sex you want to have is a good deal more important than what kind of sex that is. The best part of becoming a sexual adult is that you no longer have to restrict how you choose to define sex. We're all raised to envision sex in such painfully limited terms—"It's only sex if it involves mutual genital stimulation," or "It's only sex if it's penis-vagina intercourse; everything else is foreplay." If motherhood has taught you nothing else, we bet it has taught you that the boundaries between sensual and sexual, between emotional and physical, between self and other are simply too fluid for your eroticism to be contained in such rigid compartments. From now on, you get to define sex however you please. Here are just a few of the possibilities.

Sex isn't the be-all and end-all
Sex isn't the only way to express love, be intimate, or enjoy your body. On the other hand, every time you experience love, intimacy, or the pleasures of the body, you're in touch with your erotic nature.

> Sex is not the "be-all, end-all" in our relationship, and we know that we appreciate each other in many ways and can show that appreciation in many ways.

My husband would probably like to have sex more often (we're averaging once a month) but taking the focus off intercourse has also created a nice opportunity for doing other things, just for us, that aren't so sexual.

Sex is always changing

Once you let go of the idea that sex should follow a certain predictable script, you'll be free to appreciate how your experience changes throughout your life and from encounter to encounter.

I have fantasies of being middle-aged and alone with my husband again. Life has its cycles. Sometimes there's more room for sex, sometimes there's not. My husband and I can feel connected, emotionally and physically, with a lot or a little sex.

Sometimes sex just feels comfortable, not mind-blowing. Other times, the fact that we've been together so long makes the sex way more meaningful.

Sex is more than genital contact

Sex involves your entire body. Try keeping your genitals off limits for a week and explore the myriad other ways there are to express yourself physically. Kiss the back of her neck; massage his calves; hump each other in the car with all your clothes on. Do you have fond memories of high school make-out sessions? Then recreate them.

Every once in awhile we have a candlelit bubble bath when the kids are sleeping. We don't talk, just hold each other in the silence. It is needed.

We've learned how to be sexual with our clothes on, our genitals out of reach. In other words, we've redefined sex. We cuddle a lot and hold hands on walks. We also tell each other what we would do to each other if we had the time (like when my husband calls on his lunch hour).

Sex is more than intercourse

Kiss the tyranny of intercourse goodbye, and say hello to the anarchy of a full-bodied, imaginative sexuality. It can be challenging for heterosexual couples to replace intercourse with what's often referred to as "outercourse," because doing so forces us to throw out the rulebook. After all, intercourse supplies the defining narrative thrust to so many couples' sexual encounters—a clear beginning, middle, and end that defines the all-American, indisputable act of "doing it." Once that framework is gone, how do we know if we're at the beginning, middle, or end of an encounter? Ah, we have to decide for ourselves and then talk about it, that's how! Maybe a sexual encounter will involve genital touch, maybe not; maybe it will involve an orgasm for one or both of you, maybe not; maybe it will involve five minutes of mutual masturbation on the sofa; maybe it will involve a full day of erotic phone calls. The only prerequisite becomes pleasure.

> Do long time lapses between bouts of penis-in-vagina sex mean you are no longer in love? For us, big NO. We were/are still in love even more so, just have found other ways to be sexual together.

Sex thrives on intimacy

To sustain a sexual relationship over the long term, you need to feel a physical and emotional connection. Intimacy creates the context for the trust and acceptance that make erotic self-disclosure safe and appealing.

> Sometimes couples get in the habit of spending the evening separately. You know, like one's watching TV and the other is on the computer until bedtime, and suddenly you're trying to have sex and because you haven't seen each other, much less touched each other all day, it's not working. So, I try to make sure we spend time together, that we touch each other.

> I also touch my husband daily, as in hugging or kissing, or pats, etc. just to feel connected to him. If I can't touch him a few times, I feel lost. And he says what helps is more affection both outside and inside the bedroom—more kisses, more spontaneous affection.

Sex thrives on independence

For your eroticism to flourish, you must feel entitled to your own desires, curiosities, and preferences. Intimacy with a partner will only fuel passion if you maintain your individual identities and honor each other's differences.

Sexual compatibility isn't the ability to submerge your desires in your partner, but the ability to enjoy and balance competing desires. The balancing act you pull off as a lover and mother has the potential to enrich all your relationships.

> With children everything is a balance. So without children, you're more free to have fun and work on just the individual relationship, but with kids, you wind up working on several relationships all at the same time. It is a challenge, but in some ways feels more mature and, if done well, more bonding.

Sex is worth prioritizing

Your feelings about your body will evolve, your attitudes will shift, your fantasies will reconfigure themselves, your partners will change, your kids will grow up and leave home. Your experience of sexual pleasure is in a continuous state of flux throughout your life, but your right to pleasure stays constant. And nobody can assert that right quite as well as you can.

> We've done erotic photo shoots, and we're nude models for life drawing classes at local galleries and colleges. We play at the local nude beach in the summer (our kids go with us), and our lives, in general, include our sexual natures as part of the picture. We don't compartmentalize ourselves. Does it sound like all we think, breathe, and do is sex? Nope. He's a lawyer, and I'm a workers' comp manager for a large company. Our kids are in the third and fourth grade. My son and I play on baseball and softball teams. That's my whole point—if you don't make your erotic nature a part of your life, it won't happen, and you'll be one of those couples that says the spark ended when the kids were born. And it won't be the kids that did it. It will be your failure to keep the spark alive.

9

Sex and the
Single Mom

I f you're a single mom without a steady partner, sometimes the self-love sessions just aren't enough. You know what we're talking about: even though you work double shifts taking care of the kids, there are nights when your head hits that pillow with one all-consuming thought: "I've got to get laid." A warm body, a comforting touch, a rollicking round of sweaty sex—these are the things that rouse us out of our maternal slumbers and rejuvenate our bodies and our self-esteem.

But as you well know, wanting it and getting it are two very different things. Learning how to date again, trying to meet people, and navigating the logistical challenges around time and privacy are just a few of the obstacles littering your path to sexual communion. In this chapter, we take a look at some of the more common reasons single moms wind up sleeping alone, help you navigate the byways of dating, and offer suggestions for dealing with your kids.

By focusing on finding partners, we don't mean to imply that a single woman's solitary sexual pursuits are inadequate or inferior. On the contrary, solo erotic adventures such as masturbation and fantasy can satisfy one's carnal appetites quite nicely, and often lead to a greater understanding of and comfort with one's sexuality. But despite the appealing fact that a vibrator won't cheat on you or hog the bed, it also can't say I love you or conform to the spoon position. So although we believe you can remain sexually vital without a partner, we think intimate sexual contact makes a unique contribution to your sexual well-being and is definitely worth pursuing!

Why We Wind Up Sleeping Alone

Figuring out the who, what, why, and how of a sexual relationship can get so complicated that many single moms adopt a "why bother" attitude. As logistical challenges, legitimate fears, and seemingly insurmountable odds pile up, it's tempting simply to throw in the towel. Here are some of the more formidable forces conspiring against you, along with some suggestions for restoring a little optimism to your outlook.

My child comes first

When your days are jam-packed with work, chores, and childrearing, the last thing you need is another person demanding time and attention. After all, you only have so much to give, and by squandering it on another adult, you may feel you're depriving your kids.

> I plan on not dating until my son is two, at least. I feel that it is more important for me to be there for him than for me to be searching for some father figure that I'm sure won't show up. It's hard, but the most important thing is my child, sex or no sex.

> To me it's all about my daughter. As long as she's happy I don't need a relationship at the moment.

Impossible as it sounds, you can be emotionally and physically present for your kids and have a sex life too. Sure, it takes a little work, but you wouldn't hesitate to put that energy into finding a new job or a place to live, so why not muster some for your love life? And as for the fear that your kids will suffer—on the contrary, they'll see a happy and fulfilled mom modeling good adult relationships.

> All I can say is, don't deny yourself and your sexuality, and convince yourself that it's best to sacrifice your sex life for your children. It will always backfire on you. Plus, it gives your children a warped view of what it means to be a grown-up. If they see you making time to be with a man (or woman, as the case may be), yet not ignoring their feelings, they'll see adult relationships as a very normal part of life.

It's sometimes easier to sacrifice your needs in the name of the child's best interests rather than look at what's really preventing you from getting back on that horse. It's fine to take a break from sexual relationships, but by routinely avoiding intimacy, you actually end up doing yourself and your children a disservice.

> My advice is to get out there and get a life again ASAP. I waited so long I was almost dead by the time I got back out! I didn't really get to date until my son turned eleven and I started going out for a few hours and leaving him alone . . . it opened a door to a new life for me! Keep a social life at all costs. Pamper yourself to keep your sexuality!

Rather than postponing your needs for some indefinite time period, take another look at how a healthy sexual self-esteem can improve the quality of your life.

> Making time for yourself as a sexual person with needs and drives and desires is the single most important thing you can do for your sexual health. Keeping it separate from your children is not hard if you realize you deserve the attention and love that dating and sex can provide.

The relationship hangover

This is the "once bitten, twice shy" excuse for avoiding relationships and its tenacity should not be underestimated. Many moms got to be "single" by breaking up with their child's other parent, and they carry the baggage from that break-up for a while. Whether you've been burned by a deadbeat dad or your lesbian co-parent packed her bags, it's hard not to feel disillusioned as a result. You end up questioning your own judgment—How could the person you once loved unconditionally now be treating you or the child so badly? What's to stop you from falling for another loser?

The only cure for a hangover is time. If you've been through a nasty break-up, give yourself plenty of time to heal and don't put too much pressure on yourself to make things perfect with your ex, or to replace him or her immediately. Getting enough distance from your ex will give you a healthier perspective on that relationship and alleviate some of your guilt and anger—a perspective you'll need if you plan to continue parenting together.

My best tip for other single moms is avoiding bitterness. It spills over into every relationship you have, including with the kids and other men, and does the actual husband no harm at all since by that time he couldn't give a toss. Staying tranquil inside (thanks to psychotherapy, in my case) was the only thing that really made a difference to me.

I think it's important, if possible, to try and have some sort of positive relationship with the father so that your child can know their other half. The father of my child, if we had not had a baby, probably would've been kicked to the curb immediately. But we both have the responsibility to raise our daughter, and it's been worth the effort.

If possible, try to approach new relationships with a clean slate—it's not fair to hold one person accountable for another's shortcomings. If you need help letting go of the past, consider therapy. Above all, learn from your past relationships and be clear with future partners about just what you need and expect from them. Your self-confidence will blossom and so will your prospects for finding a partner.

Loss of a partner
The way they play it in the movies, a wife gives her soon-to-be widowed husband her heartfelt permission to remarry after she's gone. Ever notice that the dying husband rarely concerns himself with such sentiment? A woman who loses a partner is often relegated to the status of sexless widow, implying that to date again would amount to "cheating" on the dead spouse. Bucking that stereotype requires courage, a thick skin, and determination.

The death of a spouse is tragic for your entire family, but when your mourning subsides you may entertain the question of whether or not to date. Don't be surprised if you experience feelings of guilt, fear, or betrayal—these emotions are normal given the fact that you pledged your love and loyalty to someone who may be gone physically, but whose memories remain with you and your children. Take some time to reflect on what would make you happy, and if that includes companionship, pleasure, and sexual intimacy, then these are goals worth pursuing. You can seek professional help to work through any residual guilt or anxiety, join a support group, or enlist the aid and understanding of more sex-positive friends and family.

Fear and loathing

These emotions eat away at your self-image and your self-confidence, leaving you incapacitated when it comes to seeking companionship. Fear comes in many forms: fear that you'll be rejected, fear that your next partner won't be good enough, or fear that your kids won't like him or her. Loathing can manifest as general bitterness about relationships, guilt over a break-up, or negative self-image.

> I'm satisfied now, but I could never reach orgasm before because of my extreme guilt about my daughter. I felt I was a terrible mother to be having sex in the next room with someone who wasn't her father. I realize now that that's absurd, but at the time it was a very real issue for me. Once I was reassured by my partner, and I felt okay about it, I was ready to try again. And it was wonderful! I just needed to know for myself that I wasn't doing anything wrong.

It's absolutely normal to harbor insecurities, but if they become paralyzing, you need to confront them head on: What are you most afraid of? What is the worst possible scenario? What is the best? If you don't ask someone out for fear of rejection, you also miss the opportunity to experience the thrill of acceptance. Whether you fail or succeed, you can improve your self-confidence simply by taking action.

> I spent a lot of time and energy on personal ads and didn't end up finding anyone. But I'm so proud of myself for trying and feel good enough to do it again some time in the future.

The wet blankets

> My greatest difficulty was in finding peer support with regard to my need for companionship and sex. It was unbelievable how many people felt that I should forgo my feelings to save my kid.

As if you don't have enough naysaying going on inside your own head, you're probably surrounded by well-meaning, finger-wagging folk who have an opinion about every aspect of your mothering—your neighbors, relatives, other parents, church members, even some of your friends. You can expect their eyebrows will arch clear to their hairlines when they learn you want to have—or are having—sex again. As a mother your sex life becomes public property. Out come the moral yardsticks in the form of endless nosy questions: Does he have a criminal record? Did you let her sleep over when the baby was there? Don't your teenagers think it's hypocritical? Are you talking marriage? Simply imagining this cacophony of questions is enough to scare anyone celibate. And coming home from a hot date to a grand inquisition from your baby-sitter is the verbal equivalent of a cold shower.

Depending on your own personal style and your relationship to the interrogator, you can lob any number of replies, which should get the point across:

Firm politeness: "Thanks for your concern, but my personal life is private."

Feigned insult: "I can't believe you think I'd do anything that wasn't in my child's best interests!"

Sarcasm: "Yes, I'm dating a criminal, and I plan to run away with him and leave my kids on your doorstep."

Blunt and to the point: "Mind your own business."

Losing custody

The fear that we will be judged unfit mothers because of our sexual preferences deters many of us from pursuing a sex life. Single moms get blamed for so many of society's ills that adding "whoring" to our list of sins comes naturally to our accusers. The only thing worse than having the intimate details of your sex life dragged out for public scrutiny by the courts is the idea that your kids can be taken from you as a result. Sadly, the law has a checkered history of defending mothers' sexual freedoms—lesbian moms, promiscuous moms, and breastfeeding moms have all been denied custody at some point.[1] Admittedly, there's no easy solution to this problem; depending on where you live your actions might earn you the support or the disdain of your community.

It's never easy to stand up for your sexual beliefs, but by engaging in respectful, healthy relationships (with partners and children), you are actively defying the stigma associated with sexual moms. Yes, it's important to be aware of the legal precedents in your area, but it's also important not to give into a fear-based regimen of self-denial. If you find yourself anxious about the possible ramifications of your sex life, get some support. Talk to friends, a therapist, a lawyer, or other moms (go on-line where your anonymity is assured). They can help you gain some perspective and take any necessary steps to ensure that you retain custody.

The logistical limitations

It's pretty simple math: a single parent has more work to do than two parents (even assuming couples don't split child-rearing tasks evenly). Plenty of single moms will read this chapter thinking, "Yeah, how am I supposed to have a sex life when I've got meals to cook, laundry to do, work from 9-5, sports events to attend, etc.?" It's a legitimate question, and one we don't take lightly. We do our best in this book to give you some practical advice on how to free up time, get help, and manage your workload. But the simple fact is, until society prioritizes the needs of moms—including quality child care (subsidized and on-site), paid maternity and paternity leaves, job sharing, and family friendly work environments, we're never going to have enough time. So our advice to you is grab the moments you can for personal pleasure, and seize every possible opportunity to agitate for social change.

The new you

If you haven't dated since becoming a mom, you may be surprised to find that you now hold a whole new set of priorities when it comes to searching for a mate. With kids to consider, you may be more cautious when entering relationships, since any threat to your safety (or sanity) is a threat to theirs. Many mothers describe themselves as "pickier" when screening partners, and dates who don't measure up immediately to their standards or those of their kids get no second chances.

> I don't have time for games and BS so I weed people out quickly.

> I don't even consider sex unless my dates are comfortable around my boy.

Some moms up the ante by seeking parent-figures for their children.

> One of the guys I met said single moms have it harder because they're looking for a partner and a father for their kids. I recoiled at this notion, but soon realized this described my situation to a tee.

The downside of exercising so much discrimination is you may end up alone. If your expectations are set too high, you end up missing out on some pleasurable, if less cosmically significant adventures. Give yourself some room, expect to make some mistakes, and eventually you'll find a balance that works for you.

Don't try to make every relationship a "family"—not every person you date has to be a potential parent for your kids. That's way too much pressure to put on yourself, your partner, and your kids, and it's a lesson I found hard to master, at first. Once I let go, and dated who I liked, I had more satisfying relationships.

Dealing with Your Children

Even before you start dating someone regularly, it's a good idea to ponder how you want to handle your sex life with regard to your children. If you've already decided whether you want your kids to meet your partners, where you plan to have sex, and what you want your kids to know, then you won't stumble into an awkward situation unprepared, or do something you may regret later.

When should my kids meet my lover?
Most people agree that it's best not to let your lovers spend too much time with your kids until you've become more serious about your relationship. Although you may enjoy playing the field, kids form attachments easily and can be traumatized by a parade of people coming and going in their lives. Break-ups can be tougher on children than adults; this mom makes a simple case for keeping her partners separate from her kids:

Why should you AND your kids have to break up with someone?

On the other hand, don't err in the other direction and rigidly compartmentalize the pieces of your life. Kids do form attachments, but it's not as if no one ever leaves them—beloved relatives die, and friends or baby-sitters move away. Although loss can be hard on a child, it's also part of living and loving. As long as you reassure them that you're not leaving, you can help them learn that change is a very real aspect of relationships.

Your values and your circumstances will determine what approach works best for you. Some moms find that if they have the resources, it's easier to keep kids and partners separate.

> I only see the man in my life when the boys are with their father.

Others manage to strike a balance by treating their partner as they would any other "friend."

> I've always had lots of male friends, so when I meet someone new I just introduce him as "mommy's new friend." If he stays over I make sure he moves to the couch in the morning.

We appreciate the simple pragmatism of this mom's advice.

> Try not to keep your dating life too separate from your parenting life. Have enough space to enjoy, but it is important for anyone you get close to to love your children and be able to have a relationship with them.

What should my kids know about my private life?

It's possible to expend a great deal of energy trying to prevent kids from learning about sex: you can eliminate all traces of it from your home, you can avoid discussing it, and you can tell your kids they arrived on this planet via the friendly stork. But don't expect them to learn to be sexually responsible adults if no one gives them the facts, models good sexual behavior, or reassures them that their sexuality is normal.

As a parent you will have the most profound impact on your child's sexual development. You can choose to conduct your sex life, and base your child's sex education, on lies, evasiveness, and ignorance or on honesty, openness, and information. Wouldn't you rather show your children an example of a healthy intimate relationship than pretend that you have no sex life? Conducting your sex life on the sly will teach your kids that sexuality is something to hide and be ashamed of, while an honest approach will improve your relationship with your child and contribute to a healthy sexual development.

> One day I sat my kids down—they were ten and twelve—and said, "There is someone I like and he is going to stay here tonight. I don't

want to pretend to you that I'm not sexual and that I don't have a life outside of raising you, and I want you both to feel okay about whatever choices you make." My younger daughter's response was, "Remember that boy last year that I went to the dance with? Well I kissed him." She told me that she felt so much better now that I knew!

There have been many times when my boys have surprised us with a visit when we thought they were doing something with their dad. I don't throw my sexual activities in their faces but I don't lie. As they get older, I ask that they try not to just drop in when they know he is there.

I do have women stay the night, sometimes even if it's not a serious relationship. It's tough, because my son does compete for my attention, even if he likes my lover. I try to speak to him in advance, and let him know how I feel about this person, and give him some clue that she might be staying the night. If he's somewhat emotionally prepared, he reacts better. I also found the impact on both of our lives is minimized if I get up with him in the morning and do some of our routine things immediately.

Don't treat kids as your confidantes either—they are not the ones you should be sharing your relationship joys or sorrows with. And in order to avoid confusing your children, be clear about the nature of your relationship with a date or partner. Kids are fed so many stereotypes that they may harbor unrealistic expectations about your new partner. You can explain that unmarried people sleep together without any intention of marrying. You can let your kids know that the woman in your life is not a long-lost aunt, but a girlfriend who sleeps with Mommy. Similarly, don't set your partner up to play Daddy or Mommy to your child unless this truly reflects the situation.

Never ever have your child call your date Daddy/Mommy!

Where should you spend the night/have sex?

At some point, most single moms will grapple with the question of whether to invite a lover to spend the night at her home. It's definitely more convenient for you, but you need to be certain that it's safe and that you're prepared for the impact on your kids. Don't bring anyone home at any time if you harbor even the slightest reservation about having them meet your kids. If you decide that you are ready for an overnight guest, we suggest you level with your kids rather than trying to hide your lover, which can backfire.

> I would try to get the person in the house after my daughter went to bed and out before she got up which didn't always happen—not to mention kids show up in your room in the middle of the night quite unexpectedly at times. Partners also tire of being kept secret and would question my commitment.

Of course discretion and age-appropriate information should play an important part in your approach. Obviously you aren't going to let your kids watch you having sex, but you don't need to avoid having sex in your house for fear that they'll "catch you" one day either. Use the lock on the bedroom door, and prepare yourself for their questions or surprise visits. If the size and layout of your house allows it, maximize the amount of space between your bedrooms.

Younger kids are usually content with the explanation that your friend is a sleepover guest, just like the kind they have over some times. Older kids can be told that sexuality is an important part of life, requiring companionship and privacy. If your teen asks why you can have lovers sleep over and she can't, you can simply tell her that you make the rules in the house, or you can take the opportunity to talk about the maturity and responsibility necessary for sexual relationships.

> A single mom needs to make it very clear to her kids that she deserves privacy and happiness too.

You can expect a certain amount of jealousy, from your kids when the sleepovers occur (see the discussion that follows) so make sure to reassure your kids of your love for them, as this mom does.

> The first time you have that big overnight sleepover with your lover, you have to get up the next morning and really do something fun with the kids. Have a big breakfast, go to the park, do something special so they don't feel pushed to the side.

If you're trying to minimize the amount of contact your kids have with your dates, obviously it's best if everyone does not bunk under one roof. If your ex regularly takes your children, you've got a perfect scheduling opportunity for dalliances.

> I was lucky enough to have a very involved father for the first two years so I could count on a few nights a week to enjoy myself. It is nice to have at least one night to go wild—whatever your version of wild is.

Short of an ex that shares childcare responsibilites, you will be limited to brief sexual trysts unless you can hire overnight baby-sitters or arrange to have the house to yourself. When your kids are old enough, they can sleep over at their friends' houses. Likewise, you can trade overnights with another single parent. Kids can be farmed out to relatives and good friends for the occasional sleepover, or you may find a baby-sitter who will spend the night.

> What works for me for casual dating and sex is to plan activities during which my daughter is spending the night with family or friends.

> Enlist your friends! You know all those people who offer to baby-sit? Tell them point blank to not offer unless they mean it, as you WILL take them up on it. Call in those chips when you need downtime or date time or sex fling time.

Shared housing gives you live-in baby-sitters and comes with a few other perks.

> Sharing a house makes things cheaper, gives more baby-sitting resources and more options house-wide for getting privacy. It saved my life as a single parent.

How to Meet People

Once you've given yourself permission to have a sex life, the next hurdle is finding someone to have it with. How do you find that special someone to grace your bed? Take these suggestions from your fellow moms on what works for them:

Friends' referrals

As you probably discovered when trying to find child-care, legal assistance, or tradespeople, your friends can provide the most helpful referrals. Dating is no different, as your friends, relatives, and co-workers are your most valuable resources for future partners. Don't be shy about asking—let everyone know that you're interested in dating and ask them to set you up with single friends. Boldly send out a group email or casually mention it during your conversations. Once you put your mind to it, you may get quite creative.

Hot Tips: How to Meet People

- Ask friends. Let all your friends know you want to be set up.
- Join up. Groups, classes and clubs are great places to meet people.
- Go places alone. Go to adult venues (cafes, parties) alone so people know you're available.
- Go to kids' hangouts. You can meet other single parents at parks, kids' events, and day care centers.
- Place a personals ad. On-line personals are a great way to find and screen dates before meeting them.

My sister wants to throw herself a "Find Lulu a date party" where all the invitees have to bring a single friend.

After I exhausted my pool of friends, I started asking trusted business acquaintances if they had any single friends. People were most sympathetic and genuinely tried to help.

The friends' referral option has several advantages. First, your dates are pre-screened—you've less chance of ending up with a psycho—and they're actually people your friends find interesting. Second, your friends can provide a nice alternative to awkward blind dates by hosting a dinner party or planning a group outing to which you're both invited. Third, you give your friends an opportunity to unleash their inner matchmakers.

And there's no better time than when you're single to get back in touch with long lost friends. They may no longer be single, but hopefully they've made new friends that they'll want you to meet. Thanks to the Internet it's getting easier to find people you've lost track of—some schools allow alumni to post email addresses, and there are plenty of search programs to help locate individual email addresses.

Getting out

This option requires a certain commitment of time, but we think you'll benefit from pursuing activities which please you, and enjoy the time spent in the company of other adults. See the Having it All chapter for suggestions on freeing up time in your schedule.

Join a group, class, or club

Why not reap the double benefit of indulging a personal interest and exposing yourself to new people? If you've always wanted to learn French, take a class at the community college and find yourself a study partner. Book groups abound courtesy of local bookshops, schools, and libraries. If you crave a more disciplined exercise regime, sign up for a gym or an aerobics class. Join a single parenting support group.

Go places alone

Although going to parties with friends might be infinitely more enjoyable, most people who do this spend the entire time talking to people they already know. By going alone you're forced to mingle, an activity which will endear you to your hosts and earn you a few new friends. Bigger parties are often rife with somewhat intimidating circles of friends gabbing in corners, but most often you'll find that by smiling and introducing yourself, they will respect your courage and welcome you with interest.

Similarly, consider going to events like book readings, the theater, gallery openings, or shows alone since you will stand out as a single person. Look around during intermission to find other people and start a conversation by commenting on the event or performance.

Kids' hangouts

If you want to meet other single parents, you usually don't need to look any farther than your local playground.

On Sundays all the noncustodial Dads are out with their kids at the park/Chuckie Cheeses/zoo/movies/etc. Letting your kids play together is a good way to meet someone.

Neighborhood community centers, schools, and daycare facilities crave parent involvement. By getting to know other parents, single or not, you are able to tap into their networks of single friends. Even though your kids may provide the perfect ice-breaker when it comes to starting a conversation, don't spend the whole time talking about them; you're better off trying to discover common interests other than children.

Personals

To the uninitiated, personals have a bad reputation—mostly as a forum for lonely, desperate creeps who've never been able to get a date. But actually, most personals fans are just regular folk who for one reason or another want to expand their pool of potential mates. Tons of subscribers are relationship refugees reentering the dating scene, others are shy and find it difficult to socialize in person, some just don't get to meet new people very often. The people you meet through the personals don't usually have unrealistic expectations about meeting Mr. or Ms. Right every time they place or answer an ad, but they do appreciate the opportunity to cast a wide net in the hopes of one day landing the big one. And whether or not you succeed in finding a date, the whole process can help you get in touch with what you're looking for in a partner. This mom found the personals a convenient way to dip her toe back into the dating pool, as well as an effective way to screen out folks uninterested in kids.

> When I first left my ex-husband, I was pretty certain I wouldn't meet anyone until the kids were grown. I pretty much assumed that any man who heard I came complete with a set of children, all under five years old, would run screaming in the other direction. Since I didn't have time to actually go out much, where people are likely to meet, I placed a personal ad. I mentioned the children, that I had them, and that they were my priority in my personal ad. That made all the difference in the world in finding someone who was able to deal with it.

If you decide to give the personals a shot, your first step will be to decide whether you want to respond to an ad or write one of your own. Depending on what service you use, you'll either be charged to answer an ad or to place an ad. So if you're making your decision from a purely financial standpoint, find out how the billing works. If you're being charged to respond to ads, be careful as the dollars add up quickly. Unless you're swimming in money, you'll soon learn to be very selective before picking up the phone.

When you call up the personals' service to reply to an ad, you enter the box number of your candidate and then you get to hear a more extensive voice message. After this you can decide whether to leave a message of your own. The beauty of responding to ads is you have the luxury of exploring variety—do you like the clever one, the sincere one, the naughty one?

When you place an ad, you simply send in your carefully worded message and the service sets up an anonymous voicemail box for you, on which you record a more detailed message about yourself. Callers leave messages (with their phone numbers), which you call in to retrieve. You're not obligated to return calls. The advantage here is that people come to you. You're free to describe yourself or your ideal partner in any way you like, so if they listen to your laundry list of physical shortcomings or odd personality traits and still leave you a message, you've got a live one!

On-line dating services

Where do you turn when you're too old for one-night stands, too busy to join any classes, and too tired to stay up late cruising clubs? To an on-line dating service! These services, with names like Match.com and Swoon, generally operate under the same principle as the newspaper personals, but you get to advertise more detailed information, attach a photo, and communicate on-line. So if you're looking for a forty-year-old Irish Buddhist who listens to rap music and lives four blocks away (good luck!), you can search for him on-line.

Most services charge a monthly fee (with a free trial period) and offer a host of additional features like horoscopes, dating advice, discussion boards and chat rooms. The benefits of on-line dating are numerous: you can do it at night when the kids are asleep, you remain anonymous for as long as you like, you save money on babysitting, and you minimize awkward meetings. The convenience, anonymity, and pre-screening capabilities can be just the inducement for moms to reenter the dating scene.

Hot Tips: Looking for Love

Writing your personals ad

With both personals ads and dating services, it pays to put some thought into how you express yourself. A good personals ad is one that generates a few select responses.

- Be specific. If your wording is too vague you might get a lot of calls from people who turn out to have nothing in common with you. Think about what sparks your curiosity or turns you off in others' ads or profiles.
- Be yourself. Don't worry about being witty—it's hard to go wrong being sincere.
- Try not to make laundry lists of your qualities or achievements, but give examples of what you like or are interested in.
- Be honest. Don't lie about your looks or your interests—the truth will only catch up with you eventually. (Surely you've noticed that the personals world is populated by a very high proportion of "attractive" people!)
- Be open. How much emphasis you place on looks, interests, and activities is an entirely personal choice. You might not like football or body piercings, but that doesn't mean you wouldn't be compatible (sexually and otherwise) with someone who does. There's a reason that "opposites attract" is a time-honored mating sentiment. While labels are inadequate, you have to come up with some way of defining your tastes that readers can respond to. You can always take out more than one ad and try different approaches.

Meeting your date

When arranging a meeting for the first time, follow the safety tips listed in this chapter. Once you're finally face to face with your new pal, these suggestions might help break the ice.

- Try and relax. You can start by just acknowledging the awkwardness of the situation and then take it from there.
- Come prepared. If you're the shy or tongue-tied type, come prepared with some questions to get the conversation moving. Try not to monopolize the conversation, but draw your partner out with questions.
- Give it time. If you're trying to assess if there's any sexual chemistry, give it some time. Between the conversation you're both working on, and the running commentary going on in your head, your body may barely have room to breathe. It might take several dates, and some time to reflect, before you discover whether there's anything worth pursuing.

It was very difficult to make time to get out and meet people, and it was hard to find a place to get private without spending a lot of money on dinner or a hotel room or whatever (I didn't want to be bringing people home all the time). That's why I turned to the Internet—I think it's a great place to meet people. Yes, there are plenty of freaks on-line who aren't who they pretend to be. But there are plenty more people who are what they say they are. And it's easy to be forthright with people when you don't have the fear of immediate rejection and repercussion facing you—I can say what I think on the Internet, to anyone, without worrying that they're going to reject me out of hand.

As this mom reminds us, the Internet is having a hard time shaking its undeserved reputation as a place filled with "freaks," including rapists, stalkers and child-molesters. Yes, these people exist, and yes, they can and do use the Internet to ensnare potential victims, but the degree to which this occurs is vastly exaggerated by the media. We'd much rather see talk shows and newspapers take a more responsible approach to the benefits and dangers of the Internet—extolling its educational virtues and advising people on common-sense ways to protect their privacy—but we realize that wouldn't pull in the ratings during sweeps week. So we'll provide the public service announcement, and give you a brief primer on protecting your privacy.

Whether dabbling in the personals or on-line dating services, your best strategy is to follow your instincts and err on the side of caution. Use common sense when giving out information about yourself. Until you trust someone, don't give out your last name, where you live, work, etc., either in your profile or in person. Use a pseudonym or a first name only. If you're worried about what information about you is available on-line, search on your name or inquire with your service provider and ask to have personal information deleted. Complain to the site operators if you're being harassed or if someone's being creepy.

When you arrange to meet in person, follow the safety tips listed in the sidebar. Until you're confident that this individual poses no threat to you, take initiative in order to guard your privacy: make the phone calls rather than giving out your number; arrange to meet in public places to avoid being picked up at your house or at work; limit the identifying details you divulge in conversation. If you follow these precautions, you'll be just as—if not more—safe with your on-line acquaintances as you are with folks you meet at your local bookstore. And you'll have acquired valuable practice in being assertive to boot.

Hot Tips: Safety

When you find someone who piques your interest and you decide to get together, you should take a few precautions, especially if it's the first time you'll be meeting:

- Meet in a public space. Consider meeting during your lunch break; that way you have a built-in excuse to leave (and you save on baby-sitting).
- Arrive separately.
- Tell a friend where you're going and when you'll be back. Make sure you call your friend to let her or him know you've returned from the date.
- Bring a cell phone, your phone card, or change for a phone call.
- Bring plenty of money in case you need a cab to get home.
- Bring safe sex supplies in the event you are swept off your feet.
- If you're coming from out of town, don't plan to stay at your date's house, but book yourself a hotel room.

Dating Advice

When to tell your date about your kids

If you haven't told your prospective love interest about your kids before your first date, do it on your first date. There's no point in pretending that your children don't exist, and it's not fair to your date to omit this vital piece of information. Hard as it is for moms to imagine, not everyone is fond of kids.

Accept that some men will immediately avoid you because of your child and try not to take it personally.

Besides, most moms find that full disclosure helps them separate the wheat from the chaff when it comes to screening out unsuitable partners.

Be blunt, be prepared! The third sentence I say to any potential mate is (as I hold up my pager) "I love my new baby-sitter—she only pages if there's a problem." Most guys look at their watch and find some lame excuse to leave.

At the same time, be careful of dates who are too interested in your kids. You may find that it's not you they really want, but your instant family.

So far the challenge I have encountered is accurately reading people's motives. I find that people fall into three categories—those with a pregnancy/lactating mother fetish, those who want an insta-family, and those who want to be able to say they have another notch on the belt.

I keep finding people who want to treat me like I should take care of them in addition to my children.

Kids as barometers

No wonder some people run from single moms—not only do they have to pass muster with the mom, but they have to face the daunting prospect of trying to charm someone else's children. Many of the moms from our survey were quite clear that they wouldn't waste time on anyone who didn't meet little Joey or Janey's approval.

Make sure you date the kind of people you want your children around. If my kids don't like someone I'm dating—really don't like, I mean, not simply trying to get rid of them because I'm dating them—then that's the end of that guy. I trust my children's opinions.

Fortunately this mom can distinguish between the natural jealousy kids have for anyone who's competing with them for Mommy's attention and a genuine dislike. Don't allow your kids to sabotage your relationships, but do take the time to find out what they don't like about your new partner. You may discover that they have anxieties you can alleviate; for instance, letting them know they're irreplaceable in your affections and aren't expected to embrace your lover as a substitute parent could ease the strain.

We caution you not to judge partners too quickly based on their initial success (or lack of success) with your children. People who aren't accustomed to being around kids may be awkward or somewhat fearful at first, but with practice, time to relax, and the opportunity to gain confidence, they can blossom.

Jealousy

> Be patient with yourself and be patient with your lovers. They WILL get jealous of your kid. And be patient with your kids . . . they don't like these people showing up in mama's bed.

What's a mom to do when there's only so much of her to go around? With regard to your partners, it's important to be clear with them about your availability. If getting together is dependent on your schedule, make sure they're okay with this and show appreciation for their flexibility. When you're together, don't rattle on about your children, but focus on your adult time together. It's fine for you to explain that your kids come first in your life, but this shouldn't stop you from making your partner feel that she or he comes first in your personal life.

As for your kids, bear in mind that it's normal for them to be jealous of your affections for another, particularly if they haven't had to share you in a while, or if you've recently broken up with, or lost their other parent. With younger kids, explain to them that you have a special friend that you like to spend time with, just as they have favorite playmates. Older kids can be told about the importance of intimate adult relationships, and the value they have in your life. Make sure you continue to spend time alone with your kids, and don't pressure them into group outings with you and your new flame until they express interest or willingness.

Your sexual health

As one of our survey respondents puts it, "A happy mom is a good mom," and there's nothing like good health to lift your spirits. So honor your sexual health by making family planning and safer sex a routine part of your sex life. Carry condoms or dental dams with you (practice in advance if you're a little rusty) and talk openly about birth control and safe sex with your partner before you have sex. For more on this subject, see the section on safer sex in the Reinventing Sex as a Parent chapter.

A dating plan

Most single moms find that once they start dating again, they establish something of a "dating plan." This plan amounts to a philosophy incorporating what they've decided is best for themselves and their children and is used to establish boundaries with potential partners. What follows are three different types of plans, which all reflect forethought and experience.

I am very careful about whom I meet, and where I meet them. After six months of trial and error, and a few close emotional calls, I have finally evolved a dating plan. We meet several times for lunch, sometimes as many as a dozen, until a comfort level is established. Then I suggest a "family" outing. Only a couple of men have reached this level—it is an effective way to weed out those who are interested in the short-term. My theory is, my daughter needs to see a friendship develop before there is romantic involvement. Additionally, I see no point in "dating," which seems to connote romance, if this new friend and my daughter do not click.

After the birth of my second baby (as a single mom) I became very hesitant to involve myself in sexual relationships. I even swore at one point that I would not have sex again unless I was with someone I could feasibly marry and raise children with. However after the first sexual hurdle (which involved lots of crying and confusion) I discovered that sex was a need for me—to make up for the pleasure deficit and stress overload that is the burden of so many single mamas. I am not interested in relationships now, so have learned to seek protected, mutually understood one-night stands or sex with good friends at periodic intervals. I have found this to work out quite well, despite the little deep-seated southern Baptist moral voice in the back of my mind. It is safe, fulfilling, and no strings.

On my first date with the man I've been with for two and a half years, I told him that my son was my first priority no matter what, and that if he ever had me apologizing for that it would be over. Kind of heavy to lay out in the first few hours of knowing someone, but I'm glad I did. You need to have a bottom line to look to, so you can say: "I said that, I meant that, I'm going to live with it and you are too."

After reading this chapter and giving careful thought to the issues we've presented, we hope you feel confident enough to craft your own dating plan. You may find it evolves over time, so our advice is to be flexible, learn from your mistakes, and celebrate your successes!

10

Healthy Sex, Happy Families

Y ou might have noticed that most of this book focuses on how to have a good sex life in spite of your children. But we also want you to have a good sex life because of your children. When they see a happy, sexually-fulfilled mom who conducts relationships consistent with her own values, they learn to embrace sexuality as natural and to form mature relationships of their own.

Talking to your kids about sex will go a long way toward counteracting the misinformation, stereotypes, discrimination, and sex-negativity that can derail children's sex education. Unless you want your child's sexual journey to mirror Alice's trip through Wonderland—alternately nightmarish and thrilling—you need to cultivate an open and honest dialogue around sexuality.

However, you can talk to your kids about sex until you're blue in the face, but if your actions contradict your message, guess which they'll remember? When it comes to sex education, the cliché "Actions speak louder than words" rings decidedly true. Susie Bright sums up this sentiment nicely. "Be a good role model to kids. What you say is so secondary to what you do. If you want them to have a good sex life, you have a good sex life. If you want them to be comfortable talking about sex, are you? If you want them to have a good body image, have one yourself!"

This sounds great, but it ain't always easy. Maybe you feel fine about imparting age-appropriate sex information, but get queasy when your kids express any curiosity about or awareness of your own sex life. Some parents panic at the thought of kids "catching them in the act," some single parents avoid dating for fear their kids will realize they're having sex, and others evade or ignore children's questions when they get too personal. When your anxiety manifests itself to the point that you end up limiting physical affection with a partner, curbing sexual activity, or downplaying your sexuality, you've not only shortchanged your own sex life, but you've sent kids the message that adult sexuality is nonexistent, which can have devastating effects.

> Don't stop making sexuality a part of yourself because you've become a parent. Don't give your kids the unhealthy example of becoming a cold, asexual being. How are they supposed to see how a happy, healthy person relates in this world if mom and dad are examples of employees, civil servants, and parenthood, but devoid of human sexuality? How do kids learn what role sex plays in their lives when they start feeling sexual urges, themselves? I never, EVER felt comfortable with my own sexuality until after becoming a mom, because my parents never touched or kissed (not once!) in front of me. They made sex dirty, ugly, and shameful. In my opinion, that is what happens when kids are left with the impression that sex is not part of life for adults, and they have feelings and desires that are at odds with that fact. They have no clue how to deal with it.

Most parents don't intentionally choose to self-censor their sexuality, but inadvertently succumb to embarrassment, discomfort, and genuine confusion. Even if you make every effort to model sex-positive behavior, you can still be taken off guard by an ill-timed question or intrusion from you child. But a little perspective and forethought will help you enjoy your sexuality, while also consciously—and realistically—addressing its impact on your children.

Protect Your Privacy

When it comes to kids' awareness of our sex lives, we're most troubled by a vague sense that we'll offend, shock, or harm our innocent ones with some inappropriate behavior. But if you've treated sexuality as a natural and integral part of their lives, they won't view yours as unnatural. If you've answered your child's sex questions honestly, thoroughly, and nonjudgmentally, they already know that you have sex.

This is not to say that if children request explicit details about your sex life you should provide them. You can maintain your privacy without skimping on your child's education. Your son may ask if you give Dad blowjobs, to which you can reply, "That's something private between me and your dad, but if you're asking what a blowjob is, I can tell you."

Each of us has a different privacy threshold, which dictates how much personal information we feel comfortable discussing with our children. As Joani Blank points out: "It's important to legitimize people's sense of privacy—what they need and how much they need. I know moms who take baths with kids and show their genitals to their kids, but I never felt comfortable doing that. Some parents feel fine about that, but I didn't and I never felt guilty. If my daughter asked me I'd say no, just as if she'd asked, 'Can I watch you and Dad have sex?'"

When a child does or says something you find intrusive, treating this as a privacy issue rather than a sex issue will avoid sending the message that sex itself is bad or shameful. And it can have humorous results, as Susie Bright discovered: "My daughter came in without knocking while I was making out with a lover. I told her that I was making love and wanted to be alone and that I would come check on her later. I was careful to make it nonchalant, and about privacy, rather than a sex issue. But she said, 'I want to watch.' And I told her that I wasn't a TV program for her entertainment!"

When children catch you by surprise, use the opportunity to reinforce the concept of privacy. Ask your child what sorts of things she feels private about, explain that you respect her privacy, and are just asking that she respect yours. Eventually, your children will come to understand and view your sex life as something you enjoy, and they will give you the room to enjoy it.

I'm sure my nine-year-old daughter knows that my boyfriend and I share a bed when we are together. She and I have talked about sex, so she knows that we are most likely "having sex." She understands that once she is in bed when my boyfriend is over, she should not go into my bedroom without knocking. She respects my privacy and I respect hers. My boyfriend and I take care not to be loud or vulgar when she is in her room.

We don't flaunt our sexual selves in front of our kids, but they understand that a closed door means leave us alone. They know we need that time to enjoy each other, and they are comfortable with it because we don't apologize for it, we don't explain it, and we don't make a big deal of it. If they hear us, or see us kissing, we don't react like we have been caught doing something ugly or wrong.

Privacy for some parents involves eliminating any signs of their sex life, but others find that a certain openness invites children's questions and creates a more natural opportunity for them to learn about sex. For example, a child's discovery of condoms or a diaphragm in a bedside drawer might inspire a conversation about contraception and sex for pleasure. We appreciate the way that this father honestly and intentionally answers his children's questions, when it would have been much easier to respond without ever mentioning sex at all.

Some of our sexual accouterments (candles and a boom box in the bedroom) became fodder for sex education. "Why do you and Mommy have candles in your bedroom?" "Because we enjoy candlelight when we're making love." "Why do you and Mommy have a boom box in your bedroom? You never play it." "We play it when you're asleep, when we're making love. We like music then."

Live Your Values

Many of us think of values as a list of do's and don'ts which we rely upon to guide our children's development. But kids learn the most about your true values from your actions. Think about time spent at your job, with your partner, and your kids and ask yourself whether you expend more energy on greed, jealousy, self-pity, and despair, or humility, generosity, respect, and kindness. Which of these attitudes do you think make you a better lover or help you develop a healthy sexual self-esteem?

You can stimulate your own sexual creativity by tapping into the source of your passions. Figure out what brings you joy, do more of it, and you, your family, and your job will all benefit. Maybe it's dancing, listening to music, hiking, or baking exotic desserts, but if it brings you pleasure, you are in fact infusing your life with sexual energy. At the same time, take a closer look at how you've prioritized enacting your values. Make an effort to really put them into practice—not with token treats or hollow gestures—but in your daily behavior. Let a colleague run the meeting if that will convey respect, wow your partner with your thoughtfulness by doing more chores, explore generosity by volunteering. These things are what make us richer in mind, body, and spirit.

As parents, you can use your joy and generosity of spirit to imbue your children with passion. Not by lining up to buy Pokemon cards and Nintendo games, but by taking time out of your busy schedules in order to share moments of beauty and fantasy. Whether it's turning your kids on to the ballet, museums, country music, botanical gardens, architecture, cars, or cooking, when you expand children's horizons beyond animated cartoons, computer games, and plastic figurines you unlock doors to their imaginations and passions, thereby giving them the keys to creativity and eroticism.

Many parents find that their approach to sex education is an organic expression of their values. For example, these mothers believe their children are entitled to sexual fulfillment in the context of responsibility, safety, and respect, values that they impart both through words and actions.

> I have girls so I'm greatly concerned that sex be good for them from the beginning. I can't believe it took me until I was thirty-three to find my G-spot (and what a spot it is!). I also can't believe that I settled for such bland sex for so long. I want them to be so well educated about sex, for it not to be taboo, and for them to expect and get good sex when the time is right. I want them to also understand how important it is to wait until they are mature and have a mature, loving partner so their early experiences will be good and memorable and safe.

> I would like to give kids some of my own value system, which is that sexual expression is a wonderful gift, but not to be given without thought and emotion. Emotionally, I think it's important to have a level of maturity before becoming sexually active. I don't want them to regret their sexual actions (though I'm sure everyone has at least minor regrets) so I want them to give thought to things ahead of time. And the other big value is, of course, safety. My children will know about safe sex, they will know that they have nonjudgmental access to birth control, and they will know where in our home they can just go grab a condom without anyone seeing it. I think the biggest barrier to safe sex for kids is that they are so often

embarrassed to seek it, and so just go without. I don't want that for my children.

The fact that children will inevitably be exposed to sexually explicit materials such as adult magazines, soft-core advertising, erotic novels, and adult web sites disturbs many parents. But rather than attempting the impossible feat of banning sexual imagery, these two fathers use the ubiquitous presence of sexual materials as an opportunity to educate their children about their values:

> I used to write for *Playboy,* so we had the magazine around the house. I never prevented my son from looking at it. But I made sure he understood that (1) Most women don't look like Playboy models. (2) Most women have mixed emotions about not looking like that. (3) Many women feel offended by girlie magazines as an invasion of privacy and a misrepresentation of who they are. (4) The Playboy version of sex is that sex is ONLY fun, which is simplistic. The best sex comes from a loving, trusting, intimate relationship.

> I want my kids to learn that sex is much better than violence and should be more acceptable. I'd much rather them see a porno than a film showing violence as fun and appropriate. I also take them to nude beaches so they get used to real bodies (as opposed to those in *Playboy* and *Manpower*). This should help them be less judgmental of others.

We encourage you to take a closer look at how your own life reflects your values and to accept the challenge of adopting a style of sex education that allows you and your children to live and act in accordance with these values. We couldn't agree more with this mom's advice:

> Don't lie, don't be a homophobe and do not ever make it okay to be exploitative or disrespectful to others in a sexual (or nonsexual) setting. Accept your children and teach them to accept themselves and others. Sex is a wonderful thing and our children deserve to learn that.

Keep Your Perspective

How does one remain oneself in front of one's children: that is, be sexual, act sexy, have art that deals with sexuality around, yet respect what is age appropriate and right for children?

This is the heart of the matter. You may be completely committed to role modeling positive sexual attitudes for your children. You may be confident in your right to sexual pleasure, and unselfconscious in your delight of sex toys and erotica. But you, like every other mother who reads this book, will inevitably encounter those moments of nitty-gritty anxiety when your sex-positive philosophy collides with reality: Should I lock up the sex toys? Is it okay to leave that erotic photography book on the coffee table? And what should I do when the Scout troop comes over? Before you install the pad-locks, draw the curtains, and bolt the door, we encourage you to take a step back and look at the big picture.

Child-proofing your pleasure chest

We have greatly expanded our sexual oeuvre since parenthood. My partner sometimes worries about our daughter finding out about some of our nontraditional sex practices. So we keep our toys locked away. I feel that we need to establish a mutual respect with our daughter about private matters.

Like the mother quoted above, most parents choose to keep their sex accessories tucked well out of reach of their darling sons and daughters. Establishing a mutual respect for privacy is an admirable goal, but keep in mind that you won't have violated that goal if your kids spot a dildo on your bureau or catch sight of your vibrator cord sticking out from under the bed. Young children will accept your explanation that some toys are designed especially for grown-ups to enjoy while making love, and pubescent or ado-lescent children have probably known about your secret stash for some time.

Several years ago, the women-owned sex emporium Good Vibrations commemorated its fifteenth anniversary by soliciting customers' memories of their first vibrator experiences. A good 20% of these true-life tales revolved around the exciting discovery and enjoyment of a parent's vibrator. Doubtless the parents would have been horrified, but had they been more vigilant about hiding their toys, their kids would've missed out on a thrilling sexual discovery. Of course, this "don't ask, don't tell" approach can misfire:

> Hide your vibrators really well! Last year when my daughter was in first grade I got a call from the principal telling me to come in because my six-year-old was brandishing my vibrator in class!

So if you truly want to protect your privacy, get a padlock for that treasure chest!

Hiding the smut

Similarly, you may prefer keeping your sex books and videos inaccessible to your children, but we'd encourage you to think twice before you put in a secret bookcase. Quarantining sex books is just one more way to reinforce the false notion that sex somehow belongs in a separate category from the rest of life's subject matter. As for erotic art and photography, your kids live in a world in which sexual imagery is used to sell clothing, CDs, and consumer appliances—don't they deserve to know that sexual imagery is sometimes an expression of creativity and eroticism that has no price tags attached?

Of course, this line of reasoning is much easier to embrace when you're hanging an erotic lithograph on the walls of your bedroom than when you're imagining your children accidentally cueing up your latest all-anal-action video rental. It's perfectly reasonable to hide your adult videos from your kids, but we'd suggest letting them know that watching sexy videos is something adults enjoy (just as adults enjoy certain movies and TV shows that kids don't). Odds are good that your children are going to be exposed to porn, if not at your house than at someone else's. It makes sense to give them the message from an early age that adult videos aren't a secret decoder ring to the capital-T Truth about sex, but rather that they reflect adult sexuality about as much as cartoons reflect reality. As the father quoted below suggests, you can communicate your own values by letting your child know that porn is hardly a comprehensive depiction of eroticism.

> When my thirteen-year-old came home recently with a porno tape copied for him by the older brother of a friend. I didn't confiscate it or flip out. But I made sure he understood the shortcomings of porn's all-genital non-sensual approach to sex.

Honor Your Path: Nontraditional Sex Styles

> How can I be open with my children and their questions without putting ideas into their head that lead to other parents calling to chew us out?

You may be worried that the details of your sexual tastes would raise a lot of eyebrows if word got out to the PTA. Moms in nontraditional relationships can be justifiably concerned about how "out" to be (and how to be "out") in the public realm. We assume that if you're a lesbian or bisexual mom, you have a community and resources that allow you to be open about your sexuality at home. While our culture still has a long way to go toward accepting and extending full legal and economic support to gay and lesbian families, the fact is that queer families are a growing presence and political force. We were heartened by how many of our survey respondents have prioritized teaching their young children respect for diverse families. After all, the reality is that only a minority of American children are being raised in traditional families with a married mommy and daddy, so despite the weeping and wailing of political conservatives, our society is becoming more inclusive of diversity simply because it must. This said, it's still imperative that you research your legal options and take steps to safeguard your parental rights; the National Center for Lesbian Rights offers state-by-state information on legal protection (including custody, adoption, and health and financial powers of attorney).

Other alternative forms of sexual expression can be even more marginalized. Parents who are exploring alternatives to monogamy face a huge societal bias against open relationships. Nonmonogamy, sometimes referred to as polyamory, is a mutual agreement to have sexual and emotional partners outside the primary relationship. Needless to say, it hasn't exactly caught on like wildfire in our culture, where we tend to have a much higher comfort level with the notion of affairs—all that nice, familiar secrecy, lying, and cheating!

Parents who incorporate aspects of power play into their eroticism also confront a wealth of stereotypes and negative attitudes. Power exchange is one of the most common themes in sexual fantasy, and in fact, we think it's likely that many of your fellow PTA members are exploring role-playing, bondage, discipline, dominance, submission, and S/M. However, despite the fact that images of fetish fashion and bondage accessories abound in popular culture—from advertisements to music videos to cult movies—any exploration of power play that's more than skin deep is dismissed as "deviant" and "kinky."

So what impact does a nontraditional sex style have on your parenting? Not much. The privacy issues around your adult sexuality remain the same whether you're having three-minute intercourse in the missionary position in your own bedroom or heading out to an S/M play party. The ins and outs of your sexual activities are none of your kid's business; it's only relevant that you communicate your entitlement to privacy as well as pleasure. As your kids become teenagers, you may want to share bare-bones information with them (such as that you're in a nonmonogamous relationship), but again it's not necessarily appropriate to go into details.

Of course, you're also entitled (and we'd suggest obligated), to communicate realistic messages about alternative sex styles to your children. Just as a lesbian mom will want to provide her children with the coping mechanisms of self-respect, independent thinking, and awareness that ignorance and intolerance of same-sex love are still painfully widespread, a mom who enjoys power play or is nonmonogamous will want to find ways to provide her children with positive messages to counteract the misapprehensions they're bound to pick up from the world around them. This doesn't mean confiding, "Your daddy and I enjoy dominant and submissive role-playing." It could just mean saying, "Lots of adults enjoy playing dress-up or fantasy games during sex, and there's nothing wrong with that."

It's helpful to seek out and socialize with other nontraditional families, just so your children don't feel isolated. But there's no reason to create a greater charge around you and your neighbors' differences in sexual habits than you would around differences in TV-viewing, dinner menus, or standards of cleanliness. You've probably discovered just how finely tuned kids' radar can be—children quickly develop the ability to discriminate between what are and aren't appropriate topics of conversation or appropriate behaviors in different contexts. For a child, there's not that much difference between picking up that certain slang words are okay to say at your house, but would not be okay to say at Grandma's, and picking up that it's okay for Uncle Johnny to wear nothing under his chaps at the gay pride parade, but would not be okay for him to show up at the grade school holiday pageant in the same outfit. Needless to say, as the parent, it's your job to make sure that Uncle Johnny is clear on these distinctions too.

Trust Your Judgment

You've probably noticed that we eschew pat answers in favor of philoso-phizing about the variety of questions that will arise as you walk the high wire of sex-positive parenthood in a sex-negative culture. Ultimately, our pat answers would be irrelevant, because you're the only one who can decide on the appropriate balance of discretion and disclosure for your household. Your philosophy is bound to evolve over the years; in fact, you may find you take different tacks with different children depending on their personalities and your own development.

We do encourage you to trust your judgment and keep an eye on the big picture. After all, you may regret how you handle the occasional conversation, incident, or encounter related to sex—but isn't this true of other matters as well? There will always be plenty of opportunities to revisit the subject and try different approaches. If you're motivated by a sincere respect for sexual-ity and a sincere desire to communicate this respect to your children, you can't go wrong.

Authors' Note:
Finding Your Own Role Models

Your kids aren't the only ones who benefit from sex-positive role models, and you'll be well served by seeking out some of your own. Mothers deserve inspiration and validation for sexual self-expression. We need comrades to share our laughter and delight at the sexual pleasures we encounter; to share our frustration and rage at the sexual double-binds we face; and to support us in each and every radical step we take. Partners and lovers can offer valuable support (and motivation!), but we urge you to cast your net wider. When you seek a sexual role model outside the domestic realm, you reinforce the fact that sexual discourse belongs in the public domain. We need to wrest control of this discourse back from the pandering politicians, fear-mongering members of the religious right, and titillating tabloid writers who preserve a lowest-common-denominator mode of sexual expression. Wherever you find women who trust their own judgment, reject labels, and act with integrity, the odds are good that you'll find women willing to speak out about their own authentic eroticism.

You may be particularly moved by women writers, artists, and teachers.

Joan Nestle, Dorothy Allison, Susie Bright, and other lesbians who wrote courageously about love and sex were inspirational to me and key in my sexual radicalism. I just have a lot of respect for women who are out there with their sexuality and their love of sex.

You may find inspiration among friends, family, and colleagues, or guidance from women in your faith community, or workplace.

Believe it or not, I've found our church and church friends to be a valuable sex resource. Watching other couples in committed, caring relationships has encouraged me over the years.

I have a close friend who is fifty-one, to my twenty-five, who is very accepting and expressive of her sexuality. I think having a role model of her acceptance and love for herself has done wonders for my view of my own sexuality.

Trust us, once you start looking, you'll find many amazing women testifying to the power and worth of our innate sexuality. And you'll become one yourself. Don't let a natural instinct to focus your creative energies on your children prevent you from giving your erotic life its due. Your children are going to grow up and move on; if you sow the seeds of self-awareness, uncensored fantasies, sensual playfulness, and sexual independence now, you'll enjoy a harvest of pleasure that's beyond compare.

Acknowledgments

Heartfelt thanks to the hundreds of women who filled out our survey about motherhood and sex—you were our inspiration—and to our on-line pals who posted the survey: Krissy Cababa of Goodvibes.com, Heather Corinna of ScarletLetters.com, Jane Duvall of Janesguide.com, Christopher Filkins of Safersex.org, Wyyrd of HootIsland.com, and most especially Bee Lavender of hipMama.com. Our appreciation and admiration go to the courageous, out-spoken women who participated in the Sex and Parenting panel featured in SexTV's "Sexy Mamas" documentary: Helen Behar, Susie Bright, Ariel Gore, and Rachel Pepper—and to Michelle Melles for producing the show.

We are very grateful to our interview subjects, who were so generous with their time and expertise: Helen Behar, Joani Blank, Stephanie Brill of Maia Midwifery, Colette Choate, Meg Hinkley, Lisa Keller, MD, Harriet Lerner, Ann Langely, Pat Love, Andrea O'Reilly, and Maryl Walling-Millard. Thanks to Robin Brooks and Staci Haines for their referrals. We're greatly indebted to Erica Breneman, MD and Cheri Van Hoover, CNM for their prompt and thoughtful answers to a wide variety of medical questions. Needless to say, any factual errors that remain are our own.

Thanks especially to Karen Bouris, who discovered the original edition of this book and breathed new life into it, so that mothers everywhere can now enjoy it. Much love and gratitude to Becky Abbott, who first suggested we write a sex book for mothers, and to our agent, Amy Rennert. Special thanks to two of the most sex-positive parents we know: Michael Castleman for his unfailing kindness and encouragement, and Susie Bright for being an inspiration and mentor for many years. Anne is especially grateful to her sister and unofficial coparent Sheila Semans, for selflessly logging in hours of adventures, meals, and bathtimes. Cathy thanks her coworkers at The Sperm Bank of California, Jeffrey Abbott, and Becky Abbott for providing an abundance of practical and moral support during the writing of this book. Most of all, we send kisses to our own kids, Roxanne, Lily, and Maurice, who make us proud to be sexy moms.

Notes

Chapter 1

1. Barbara Ehrenreich and Deirdre English, *For Her Own Good* (New York: Doubleday, 1978), 244.

2. Susie Bright, *Full Exposure* (San Francisco, CA: HarperSF, 1999), 20.

3. Michie Mee, "Sexy Mamas," SexTV, February 2000.

Chapter 2

1. Laura Fraser, "Body Love, Body Hate," *Glamour*, October 1998, 281.

2. Ibid., 282–283.

3. Quoted in an interview with Moira Brenna, "The Opposite of Sex," *Ms.*, August/September 1999, 64.

4. Marty Klein, PhD and Riki Robbins, PhD, *Let Me Count the Ways: Discovering Great Sex Without Intercourse* (New York: Jeremy P. Tarcher/Putnam, 1998), 147.

5. Joan Jacobs Brumberg, *The Body Project: An Intimate History of American Girls* (New York: Random House, 1997), 212.

6. *The Works of Aristotle the Philosopher, in Four Parts*, quoted in John D'Emilio and Estelle B. Freedman, *Intimate Matters: A History of Sexuality in America* (New York: Harper & Row, 1988), 46.

Chapter 3

1. S.A. Tissot, quoted in Walter Kendrick, *The Secret Museum: Pornography in Modern Culture* (New York: Viking, 1987), 89.

2. According to the nineteenth-century American health reformer John Kellogg, who promoted clean living, self-restraint, and a bland diet (like the cereals he invented).

3. Deidre English and Barbara Ehrenreich, *For Her Own Good* (New York: Doubleday/Anchor, 1978), 123.

4. Memorable words from *All My Children's* Tad Martin while advising an acquaintance to get over his troubled childhood.

Chapter 4

1. Barbara Smuts, quoted in Natalie Angier, *Woman: An Intimate Geography* (New York: Houghton Mifflin, 1999), 335.

2. Associated Press report, "Study Finds Dysfunction in Sex Lives Is Widespread," *New York Times,* 9 February 1999.

3. Natalie Angier, "Science Is Finding Out What Women Really Want," *New York Times,* 13 August 1995. Ellen Laan also makes an explicit connection between her results and the fact that women sometimes lubricate vaginally during rape. Obviously, this automatic, physiological response doesn't indicate that women are turned on by being raped.

4. Angier, 200–201.

5. Jack Morin, PhD, *The Erotic Mind* (New York: HarperCollins, 1995), 6.

Chapter 6

1. John Gottman and Nan Silver, *Seven Principles for Making Marriages Work* (New York: Three Rivers Press, 1999).

Chapter 7

1. Jack Morin, PhD, *The Erotic Mind* (New York: HarperCollins, 1995), 268.

2. Lenore Tiefer, *Sex Is Not a Natural Act & Other Essays* (Boulder, CO: Westview Press, 1995), 11–12.

3. Sheila Kitzinger, *Ourselves as Mothers: The Universal Experience of Motherhood* (Reading, PA: Addison-Wesley, 1994), 7.

4. See Sarah Blaffer Hrdy, *Mother Nature: A History of Mother, Infants, and Natural Selection* (New York: Random House, 1999) for a well-balanced discussion of how mothers are not the only individuals capable of meeting their infant's needs.

5. Carolyn Pape Cowan and Philip A. Cowan, *When Parents Become Partners* (Mawah, NJ: Lawrence Erlbaum Associates, 1992).

6. Harriet Lerner, *The Mother Dance* (New York: HarperCollins, 1999) 37.

7. A summary of recent studies on the subject of parental division of labor can be found in Raymond Chan, Risa Brooks, Barbara Raboy, and Charlotte Patterson, "Division of Labor Among Lesbian and Heterosexual Parents: Associations with Children's Adjustment," *Journal of Family Psychology,* 12, 3 (1998): 402–419. The researchers found that while "both lesbian and heterosexual couples reported relatively equal divisions of paid employment and of household and decision-making tasks, lesbian biological and nonbiological mothers shared childcare tasks more equally than did heterosexual parents."

8. Ibid., 403.

9. Patricia Love, EdD and Jo Robinson, *Hot Monogamy* (New York: Dutton, 1994), 70.

10. In discussing loss of desire in long-term relationships, Morin comments, "I haven't seen a couple—nor have any of the colleagues I've informally surveyed—who were able to rebuild a sexual connection after they had stopped thinking of each other in an erotic way for five or more years." *The Erotic Mind,* 283.

11. See Alan R. Hirsch, *Scentsational Sex: The Secret to Using Aromas for Arousal* (Los Angeles" Element Books, 1998).

Chapter 8

1. Natalie Angier, "In the History of Gynecology, a Surprising Chapter," *The New York Times,* 23 February 1999, discussing Rachel Maines, *The Technology of Orgasm: 'Hysteria,' the Vibrator and Women's Sexual Satisfaction* (Baltimore, MD: Johns Hopkins Press, 1999).

2. Per a 1997 press release from the Lawrence Research Group, reporting results of The National Sexual Health Survey of almost 8000 Americans ages 18 to 90. The general survey was funded by National Institute of Mental Health, and the sex toy questions were funded by the Lawrence Research Group, publisher of the Xandria Collection catalog.

3. Sheila Kitzinger, *Ourselves as Mothers: The Universal Experience of Motherhood* (Reading, PA: Addison-Wesley, 1994), 11.

Chapter 9

1. Lauri Umansky, "Breastfeeding in the 1990s: The Karen Carter Case and the Politics of Maternal Sexuality," *Bad Mothers: The Politics of Blame in Twentieth Century America* Molly Ladd-Taylor and Lauri Umansky, editors, (New York: New York University Press, 1998).

Recommended Reading

Parenting

Bing, Elizabeth and Colman, Libby, PhD. *Laughter and Tears: The Emotional Life of New Mothers*. New York: Henry Holt, 1997. From the first hours after giving birth through the end of the first year, this book covers the highs and lows of the transition to motherhood.

Clunis, D. Merilee and Green, G. Dorsey. *The Lesbian Parenting Book: A Guide to Creating Families and Raising Children*. New York: Seal Press, 1995. Two lesbian therapists (and parents) cover the how-tos of everything from conception and adoption to "coming out" to children and families and addressing homophobia in age-appropriate ways.

Engber, Andrea and Klungness, Leah. *The Complete Single Mother*. Cathedral City, CA: Adams Publishing, 1995. The founder of the National Organization of Single Mothers dishes up practical advice on time and money management, talking about a missing parent, child support, adoption, legal concerns, dating, and finding support.

Gore, Ariel. *The Hip Mama Survival Guide*. New York: Hyperion, 1998. A fast-paced, funny, and nontraditional guide to pregnancy, childbirth, and parenting.

Gore, Ariel. *The Mother Trip*. New York: Seal Press, 2000. A collection of short personal essays from the inimitable founder of *Hip Mama* magazine.

Kitzinger, Sheila. *The Year after Childbirth: Enjoying Your Body, Your Relationships, and Yourself in Your Baby's First Year*. New York: Charles Scribner's Sons, 1994. A sympathetic guide to weathering the physical, emotional, and situational changes postpartum.

Martin, April. *The Lesbian and Gay Parenting Handbook: Creating and Raising Our Families*. New York: HarperCollins, 1993. Written by a psychotherapist (and mom), this affirming and comprehensive guide is filled with resources and first-person stories.

Mattes, Jane. *Single Mothers by Choice*. New York: Random House, 1994. The founder of this national support group discusses the options, pitfalls, and rewards of choosing single motherhood.

Wates, Michelle and Jade, Rowen, editors. *Bigger Than The Sky: Disabled Women On Parenting*. North Pomfret, VT: The Women's Press/Trafalgar Square, 1999. Disabled women speak out about their fight for the right to be mothers.

Talking to Children about Sex and Family Building

Basso, Michael J. *The Underground Guide to Teenage Sexuality: An Essential Handbook for Today's Teens and Parents*. Minneapolis: Fairview Press, 1997. Answers teens' questions about health and sexuality.

Bernstein, Anne, PhD. *Flight of the Stork: What Children Think (and When) About Sex and Family Building* Indianapolis: Perspectives Press, 1994. Explains how children organize information on sex and reproduction at different developmental stages.

Haffner, Debra. *From Diapers to Dating: A Parent's Guide to Raising Sexually Healthy Children*. New York: Newmarket Press, 2000. Written by the president of Sexuality Information and Education Council of the US.

Hickling, Meg, RN. *Speaking of Sex*. Kelowna, BC: Northstone Publishing, 1996. Thorough, engaging, and often humorous sex advice for parents of kids of all ages.

Martens Miller, Patricia. *Sex Is Not a Four-Letter Word! Talking with Your Children Made Easier*. New York: Crossroad Publishing Company, 1994. Places sexuality education and acceptance of all sexual orientations within a religious (Judeo-Christian), ethical framework.

Melberg Schwier, Karin and Hingsburger, David. *Sexuality: Your Sons and Daughters With Intellectual Disabilities*. Baltimore: Paul H Brookes Publishing Co, 2000. A guide to interacting with children of any developmental ability in ways that encourage self-esteem, appropriate behavior, identification of abuse, and the development of relationships.

Moglia, Ronald Filiberti, EdD and Knowles, Jon, editors. *All About Sex: A Family Resource on Sex and Sexuality*. New York, NY: Planned Parenthood Federation of America, 1997. Family sourcebook on sexuality and family planning.

Quackenbush, Marcia and Villareal, Sylvia, MD. *Does AIDS Hurt? Educating Young Children About Aids*. Scotts Valley, CA: ETR Associates, 1992. A guide to discussing AIDS in age-appropriate ways for teachers, parents, and health care providers.

Ruskai Melina, Lois. *Making Sense of Adoption: A Parent's Guide*. New York: Harper & Row, 1989. A classic guide to navigating adoption that includes material on how to discuss "where I came from" with children adopted or conceived through assisted reproduction.

Sex Information and Enhancement

Women's Sexuality

Blank, Joani, editor. *Femalia*. San Francisco: Down There Press, 1993. Over thirty full-color photographs of women's genitals.

Boston Women's Health Collective. *Our Bodies, Ourselves for the New Century: A Book by and for Women*. New York: Simon & Schuster/Touchstone, 1998. Covers all aspects of general and sexual health.

Brown Doress, Paula and Laskin Siegal, Diana. *New Ourselves, Growing Older*. New York: Simon & Schuster/Touchstone, 1996. Specific to the concerns of women over forty.

Corinne, Tee. *Cunt Coloring Book*. Tallahassee, FL: Naiad Press, 1989. Line drawings of women's genitals—for you to color in.

Dodson, Betty. *Sex For One: The Joy of Selfloving*. New York: Crown Publishers/Harmony Press, 1996. A thorough—and thoroughly infectious—guide to the joys of masturbation, illustrated with Dodson's erotic line drawings.

Federation of Feminist Women's Health Centers. *New View of a Woman's Body*. Los Angeles: Feminist Health Press, 1991. This self-help classic includes color photographs of women's genitals.

Garfield Barback, Lonnie. *For Yourself: The Fulfillment of Female Sexuality*. New York: Penguin Group/Signet, 1975. The classic guide to achieving orgasm and enhancing sexual responsiveness.

Haines, Staci. *The Survivor's Guide to Sex: How to Have an Empowered Sex Life After Child Sexual Abuse*. San Francisco: Cleis Press, 1999. How to rebuild a fulfilling sex life, identify dissociation, handle triggers, and cultivate sexual pleasure.

Heart, Mikaya. *When the Earth Moves: Women and Orgasm*. Berkeley: Celestial Arts/Ten Speed Press, 1998. Tips on enjoying and enhancing the experience of orgasm, with quotes from hundreds of women.

Heiman, Julia and LoPiccolo, Joseph. *Becoming Orgasmic*. New York: Simon & Schuster/Fireside, 1986. A structured series of exercises designed for women who have never had orgasms.

Kahn Ladas, Alice, Whipple, Beverly and Perry, John D. *The G Spot and Other Recent Discoveries about Human Sexuality*. New York: Bantam Doubleday Dell, 1982. The book that launched a thousand curious fingers.

Taormino, Tristan. *The Ultimate Guide to Anal Sex for Women*. San Francisco: Cleis Press, 1997. Covers all aspects of anal eroticism.

White, Evelyn C. *The Black Women's Health Book: Speaking for Ourselves*. New York: Seal Press, 1994. Over fifty African American women address a variety of issues affecting their health, with some discussion of sexual health.

Winks, Cathy. *The Good Vibrations Guide: the G-spot*. San Francisco: Down There Press, 1999. Information on the G-spot, female ejaculation, and tips and techniques for pleasurable exploration.

Men's Sexuality

Bechtel, Stefan and Stains, Laurence Roy. *Sex: A Man's Guide*. Emmaus, PA: Rodale Press, 1996. Well-researched information on a range of topics.

Casteleman, Michael. *Sexual Solutions: A Guide for Men and the Women Who Love Them*. New York: Simon & Schuster/Touchstone, 1983. Well-written information and advice geared to men in heterosexual relationships.

Zilbergeld, Bernie. *The New Male Sexuality: The Truth about Men, Sex and Pleasure*. New York: Bantam Books, 1992. Practical advice on common sexual concerns.

Manuals and More

Blank, Hanne. *Big, Big Love: A Sourcebook on Sex for People of Size and Those Who Love Them*. Oakland, CA: Greenery Press, 2000. A wonderful affirmation of fat people's sexuality, and an excellent resource for anyone who has body image issues related to size.

Blank, Joani with Whidden, Ann. *Good Vibrations: The New Complete Guide to Vibrators*. San Francisco: Down There Press, 2000. Learn how to select, enjoy, and introduce your partner to a vibrator.

Block, Joel D., PhD and Crain Bakos, Susan. *Sex Over Fifty*. Englewood, NJ: Prentice Hall Press, 1999. A thorough guide, including tips, techniques, and health information.

Corn, Laura. *101 Nights of Great Romance* (1996); *101 Great Quickies* (1997); *101 Nights of Great Sex* (1995). Santa Monica, CA: Park Avenue Press. Unseal each page of these creative heterosexual couples' books to discover suggestions for exploring sensuality and building intimacy.

Cornog, Martha. *The Big Book of Masturbation*. San Francisco: Down There Press, 2003. A look at the historical and cultural attitudes toward masturbation.

Dodson, Betty. *Orgasms for Two*. New York: Harmony Books, 2002. Sex guide geared toward enhancing partner sex.

Joannides, Paul. *Guide to Getting It On!: A New and Mostly Wonderful Book About Sex*. Waldport, OR: Goofy Foot Press, 1998. Covers a variety of sexual interests and activities with enthusiasm and humor.

Keesling, Barbara. *Talk Sexy to the One You Love*. New York: HarperCollins, 1996. Learn to create and enjoy an erotic vocabulary.

Klein, Marty, PhD and Robbins, Riki, PhD. *Let Me Count the Ways: Discovering Great Sex Without Intercourse*. New York: Jeremy P. Tarcher/Putnam, 1998. Exposes the "cult of intercourse" for the oppressive, sex-negative monolith that it is, and offers tips for exploring your own unique sexuality.

Love, Dr. Patricia and Robinson, Jo. *Hot Monogamy: Essential Steps to More Passionate, Intimate Lovemaking*. New York: Penguin/Plume, 1994. Exercises for monogamous couples who want to improve sexual intimacy and technique.

Morin, Jack, PhD. *Anal Pleasure and Health*. San Francisco: Down There Press, 1998. The foremost guide to enjoying anal stimulation.

Morin, Jack, PhD. *The Erotic Mind: Unlocking the Inner Sources of Sexual Passion and Fulfillment*. New York: HarperCollins, 1995. A fascinating exploration of the nature of arousal that guides readers to uncover what really turns them on and why.

Moser, Charles, PhD, MD. *Health Care Without Shame*. Oakland, CA: Greenery Press, 1999. Geared primarily toward those with alternative sexual lifestyles, this book offers invaluable advice on talking to health care providers about sexuality.

Newman, Felice. *The Whole Lesbian Sex Book*. San Francisco: Cleis Press, 1999. A comprehensive sex manual for women who love women.

Queen, Carol. *Exhibitionism for the Shy*. San Francisco: Down There Press, 1995. Tips for dressing up, showing off, talking sexy, and communicating your desires with a partner.

Reichman, Judith, MD. *I'm Not in the Mood: What Every Woman Should Know About Improving Her Libido*. New York: William Morrow & Co, 1998. Highlights the effect of hormones—specifically testosterone—on libido, and discusses physiological as well as emotional factors in offering solutions to waning desire.

Semans, Anne. *The Many Joys of Sex Toys*. New York: Broadway Books, 2004. Easy ways to enhance twenty-five popular sexual techniques with sex toys.

Semans, Anne and Winks, Cathy. *The Good Vibrations Guide to Sex*. San Francisco: Cleis Press, 2002. The best, most comprehensive sex manual ever written—trust us!

Semans, Anne and Winks, Cathy. *The Woman's Guide to Sex on the Web*. San Francisco: HarperSF, 1999. Annotated guide to over two hundred of the best sex information and entertainment web sites created by and for women.

Sundahl, Deborah. *Female Ejaculation and the G Spot*. Alameda, CA: Hunter House, 2003. Thorough discussion of female ejaculation and the G Spot.

Taylor, Emma and Sharkey, Lorelei. *The Big Bang*. New York: Plume, 2003. Very hip, nonjudgmental sex guide from the sex experts at Nerve.com.

Wheeler, Susan and Crabtree, Linda. *Intimate Resources for Persons with Disabilities*. St. Catharines, Canada: Sureen Publishing, 1999. An extensive collection of informational, educational, and consumer resources.

Cultural Studies/Sexual Politics

Angier, Natalie. *Woman: An Intimate Geography*. Boston: Houghton Mifflin, 1999. A fascinating, wide-ranging excursion through the biology of the female body.

Blaffer Hrdy, Sarah. *Mother Nature: A History of Mothers, Infants, and Natural Selection*. New York: Random House, 1999. A renowned feminist anthropologist and primatologist examines how millennia of evolutionary forces have shaped maternal behaviors and strategies.

Bright, Susie.
Mommy's Little Girl: Susie Bright on Sex, Motherhood, Pornography, and

Cherry Pie. New York: Thunder's Mouth Press, 2004

Full Exposure: Opening up to Your Sexual Creativity and Erotic Expression. San Francisco: HarperSF, 1999.

Susie Bright's Sexual State of the Union. New York: Simon & Schuster, 1997.

Susie Bright's Sexwise. San Francisco: San Francisco: Cleis Press, 1995.

Susie Bright's Sexual Reality: A Virtual Sex World Reader. San Francisco: Cleis Press, 1992.

Susie Sexpert's Lesbian Sex World. San Francisco: Cleis Press, 1990.

All of Susie Bright's collections of essays will make you laugh, provoke you, pique your curiosity, and—best of all—inspire you to think about sexuality in a whole new way.

Burke, Phyllis. *Gender Shock: Exploding the Myths of Male and Female.* New York: Anchor Books/Doubleday, 1996. A provocative and highly readable attack on our rigid gender system.

D'Emilio, John and Freedman, Estelle B. *Intimate Matters: A History of Sexuality in America,* second edition. Chicago: University of Chicago Press, 1997. A compelling read about the evolution of American sexual attitudes over the past four centuries.

English, Deidre and Ehrenreich, Barbara. *For Her Own Good: 150 Years of the Experts' Advice to Women.* New York: Anchor Books/Doubleday, 1978. Written with wit and verve, this classic of women's history reveals the toll medical "expertise" has taken on women's bodies and minds.

Jacobs Brumberg, Joan. *The Body Project: An Intimate History of American Girls.* New York: Random House, 1997. Details how and why American girls have less self-esteem and more dissatisfaction with their bodies now than one hundred years ago.

Tiefer, Lenore. *Sex Is Not a Natural Act.* Boulder, CO: Westview/Perseus Books, 1995. A collection of short, smart essays that skillfully expose the assumptions underlying our cultural construction of sexuality.

Resources

Sexuality Resources, Organizations, and Web Sites

Sex Information and Enhancement On-line

Clean Sheets
http://www.cleansheets.com
A quality sex zine that's equal parts erotica and commentary.

Clitical
http://www.clitical.com
An excellent general resource on female sexuality, with an active community and a charming webmistress, who is also a mom.

Erotic Readers and Writers Association
http://www.erotica-readers.com
An excellent forum for women and men interested in writing, reading or talking about erotica, ERA includes links to selected erotica sites.

Jane's Net Sex Guide
http://www.janesguide.com
Jane is the Ralph Nader of on-line adult commerce: she reviews hundreds of adult sites, provides consumer tips, and exposes fraudulent practices. And she's a mom.

Scarlet Letters: The Journal of Femmerotica
http://www.scarletletters.com
High-quality, high-spirited erotica, articles, and advice from a women-run site.

Society for Human Sexuality
http://www.sexuality.org
The largest on-line archive of sexuality materials, sponsored by the University of Washington, is a goldmine of useful information.

SusieBright.com
http://www.susiebright.com/forum
Susie's site features excerpts from her sex-positive articles and essays.

Sexual and Physical Health

American Social Health Association
PO Box 13827
Research Triangle Park, NC 27709
Phone: (919) 361-8400
Fax: (919) 361-8425
http://www.ashastd.org
A private, nonprofit organization, ASHA provides up-to-date information on STDs via its telephone hotlines and web site. The well-maintained site has an exceptional links page.

The Body: An AIDS and HIV Information Resource
http://www.thebody.com
Posts articles and information about safer sex, including a forum where questions from HIV-positive moms are answered by medical experts in the fields of Pediatric AIDS and HIV treatment.

Circumcision Information and Resource Pages
http://www.cirp.org
Includes medical and historical articles, as well as information for parents and educators.

Dimensions Magazine
PO Box 640
Folsom, CA 95763-0640
Phone: (916) 984-9947
http://www.dimensionsmagazine.com
This print magazine and web site explores sexuality and relationships for BBW (big, beautiful women) and their admirers.

Gender Issues
http://songweaver.com/gender
A directory site with extensive links to transgender resources and information.

HIV InSite: Gateway to AIDS Knowledge
http://hivinsite.ucsf.edu
The University of California San Francisco's comprehensive resource site includes a section on pregnancy, childbirth, and HIV.

Intersex Society of North America
4500 9th Ave. NE, Suite 300
Seattle, WA 98105
Phone: (206) 633-6077
http://www.isna.org
National organization with the goal of ending shame, secrecy, and unwanted genital surgeries for people born with atypical sex anatomy.

RAINN (Rape, Abuse & Incest National Network)
635-B Pennsylvania Ave. SE
Washington, DC 20003
(800) 656-HOPE
http://www.rainn.org
Sponsors the only national hotline for survivors of sexual assault; free confidential counseling round-the-clock; web site with statistics and resources.

Safer Sex Page
http://www.safersex.org
This friendly, comprehensive site takes a multimedia approach to sex education and dispenses information on risk management, birth control, and every kind of safer sex supply.

SexualHealth.com
http://www.sexualhealth.com
An excellent site offering a wide range of sexuality resources for people with physical disabilities, illness, or other health related problems.

Hotlines

Sexual Health

- Emergency Contraception Hotline (800) 584-9911
- National Abortion Federation Hotline (800) 772-9100
- AIDS/Center for Disease Control National Hotline (800) 342-AIDS
  Spanish (800) 344-7432
  For hearing impaired (800) 243-7889
- National STD Hotline (800) 227-8922

- American Social Health Association Hotline (800) 230-6039
- National Herpes Hotline (919) 361-8488

Sexual Abuse and Domestic Violence

- Domestic Violence Hotline (800) 799-SAFE
- National Child Abuse Hotline (800) 4-A-CHILD
- RAINN (Rape Abuse & Incest National Network) (800) 656-HOPE

Gay and Lesbian

- National Gay and Lesbian Hotline (888) 843-4564

Information

- San Francisco Sex Information (415) 989-7374
- Seattle Sex Information (206) 328-7711

Parenting Resources, Organizations, and Web Sites

Mothers' Resources

American College of Nurse Midwives
818 Connecticut Avenue, NW, Suite 900
Washington, DC 20006
Phone: (202) 728-9860
Fax: (202) 728-9897
http://www.midwife.org
The web site for this national organization has extensive links related to pregnancy, medical issues, women's health, and parenting.

Depression After Delivery
POB 1282
Morrisville, PA 19067
Phone: (800) 944-4PPD
Phone: (215) 295-3994
Resource for women with postpartum depression.

Hip Mama
http://hipmama.com
The on-line version of this progressive zine features provocative essays and interviews related to parenting and teen motherhood—and is home to thriving discussion boards.

National Center for Education in Maternal and Child Health
2115 Wisconsin Avenue NW, Ste. 601
Washington, DC 20007-2292
Phone: (202) 784-9970
http://www.ncemch.org
Publishes research and public policy recommendations.

National Center for Lesbian Rights
870 Market Street, #570
San Francisco, CA 94102
Phone: (415) 392-6257
Phone: (800) 528-NCLR
http://www.nclrights.org
NCLR advances the rights and safety of lesbians and their families through litigation, public policy advocacy, free legal advice and counseling, and public education.

Parents with Disabilities On-line!
http://www.disabledparents.net
A one-stop resource for parents with physical disabilities, this site has excellent annotated links and is the home of the Parent Empowerment listserve.

ParentsPlace
http://www.parentsplace.com
Offers countless discussion boards on a multitude of topics, including donor insemination and single parenting.

Single Mothers By Choice
PO Box 1642, Gracie Square Station
New York, NY 10028
Phone: (212) 988-0093
http://www.singlemothers.org
National organization with regional chapters.

Shopping Guide

Specialty

Corolle dolls (French anatomically correct baby dolls)
http://www.corolledolls.com
Corolle's web site lists retail outlets throughout the US.

Nolo Press
950 Parker Street,

Berkeley, CA 94710
Phone: (800) 728-3555
http://www.nolo.com
Publishes legal self-help books, including guides for lesbian and gay couples, unmarried couples, and couples building child custody agreements.

Tapestry Books
PO Box 6448
Hillsborough, NJ 08844
Phone: (800) 765-2367
http://www.tapestrybooks.com
One-of-a-kind catalog of books on adoption, infertility, and assisted reproduction—for adults and children.

Sex Toys, Books, and Videos

Blowfish
(Mail order only)
PO Box 411290
San Francisco, CA 94141
Phone: (800) 325-2569
Fax: (415) 252-4349
http://www.blowfish.com

Come as You Are
(Mail order only)
701 Queen Street West
Toronto, Ontario M6J 1E6 Canada
Phone: (416) 504-7934
Fax (416) 504-7490
http://www.comeasyouare.com

Eve's Garden
(Retail store and mail order)
119 W. 57th Street, #420
New York, NY 10019-2383
Phone: (800) 848-3837
http://www.evesgarden.com

Focus International
(Mail order only; sexual self-help videos)
1160 East Jericho Turnpike
Huntington, NY 11743
Phone: (800) 955-0888

http://www.focusint.com

Good Vibrations
(Mail order only)
938 Howard Street, #101
San Francisco, CA 94103
Phone: (800) 289-8423
http://www.goodvibes.com

(Retail stores)
1210 Valencia Street
San Francisco, CA 94110
Phone: (415) 974-8980

1620 Polk Street (at Sacramento Street)
San Francisco, CA 94109
Phone: (415) 345-0400

2504 San Pablo Avenue
Berkeley, CA 94702
Phone: (510) 841-8987

Grand Opening
(Mail Order)
318 Harvard Street, #32
Brookline, MA 02146
Phone: (617) 731-2626
http://www.grandopening.com

(Retail Stores)
318 Harvard Street, #32
Brookline, MA 02146
Phone: (617) 731-2626

8442 Santa Monica Blvd.
West Hollywood, CA 90069
Phone: (323) 848-6970

Libida
(Mail order only)
1094 Revere Ave., #A54
San Francisco, CA 94124
Phone: (415) 822-3035
http://www.libida.com

Safe Sense
(Mail order only; primarily safer sex supplies)
WWWarehouse, Inc.
2015 Polk Street
San Francisco, CA 94109
Phone: (888) 702-6636
http://www.safesense.com

Toys in Babeland
(Mail order)
Phone: (800) 658-9119
http://www.babeland.com

(Retail Stores)
94 Rivington Street
New York, NY 10002
Phone: (212) 375-1701

43 Mercer Street
New York, NY 10013
Phone: (212) 966-2120

707 E. Pike Street
Seattle, WA 98122
Phone: (205) 328-2914

The Xandria Collection
(Mail order only)
165 Valley Drive
Brisbane, CA 94005
Phone: (800) 242-2823
http://www.xandria.com

A Woman's Touch
(Retail store and mail order)
600 Williamson Street
Madison, WI 53703
Phone: (608) 250-1928
http://www.a-womans-touch.com

New World Library is dedicated to publishing books and other media that inspire and challenge us to improve the quality of our lives and the world.

We are a socially and environmentally aware company, and we strive to embody the ideals presented in our publications. We recognize that we have an ethical responsibility to our customers, our staff members, and our planet.

We serve our customers by creating the finest publications possible on personal growth, creativity, spirituality, wellness, and other areas of emerging importance. We serve New World Library employees with generous benefits, significant profit sharing, and constant encouragement to pursue their most expansive dreams.

As a member of the Green Press Initiative, we print an increasing number of books with soy-based ink on 100 percent postconsumer-waste recycled paper. Also, we power our offices with solar energy and contribute to nonprofit organizations working to make the world a better place for us all.

Our products are available
in bookstores everywhere.
For our catalog, please contact:

New World Library
14 Pamaron Way
Novato, California 94949

Phone: 415-884-2100 or 800-972-6657
Catalog requests: Ext. 50
Orders: Ext. 52
Fax: 415-884-2199
Email: escort@newworldlibrary.com

To subscribe to our electronic newsletter, visit
www.newworldlibrary.com